SAVING CONGRESS FROM ITSELF

SAVING
CONGRESS
FROM ITSELF

EMANCIPATING THE STATES &
EMPOWERING THEIR PEOPLE

★

BY JAMES L. BUCKLEY

ENCOUNTER BOOKS
New York · London

First American edition published in 2014 by Encounter Books,
an activity of Encounter for Culture and Education, Inc.,
a nonprofit, tax-exempt corporation.
Encounter Books website address: www.encounterbooks.com

Manufactured in the United States and printed on
acid-free paper. The paper used in this publication meets
the minimum requirements of ANSI/NISO Z39.48–1992
(R 1997) (*Permanence of Paper*).

FIRST AMERICAN EDITION

LIBRARY OF CONGRESS CATALOGING-IN-PUBLICATION DATA
Buckley, James Lane, 1923–
Saving Congress from itself : emancipating the states and empowering their people /
by James L. Buckley.
pages cm
Includes bibliographical references and index.
ISBN 978-1-59403-774-0 (hardcover : alk. paper) — ISBN 978-1-59403-775-7 (ebook)
1. Federal government—United States. 2. United States. Constitution. 3. United States.
Congress. 4. Intergovernmental fiscal relations. 5. Sovereignty. I. Title.
JK325.B84 2014
320.473'049—dc23
2014019242

PRODUCED BY WILSTED & TAYLOR PUBLISHING SERVICES
Copy editor Jennifer Brown
Designer and compositor Nancy Koerner

★

For my brother

FERGUS REID BUCKLEY

IF MEN WERE ANGELS,
no government would be necessary.
If angels were to govern men, neither external nor
internal controls on government would be necessary.
In framing a government that is to be administered
by men over men, the great difficulty lies in this:
you must first enable the government to control the governed;
and in the next place oblige it to control itself.

—JAMES MADISON
Federalist No. 51

★

Contents

Introduction

The United States faces two major problems today: runaway spending that threatens to bankrupt us and a Congress that appears unable to deal with long-term problems of any consequence. A significant source of each is a category of federal expenditures that has somehow escaped the notice it deserves. I refer to federal grants to state and local governments that have soared from $24.1 billion in 1970 to an estimated $640.8 billion in 2015. Grants-in-aid programs now absorb major portions of congressional time, thereby diverting Congress from its core national responsibilities, and they expend extraordinary amounts of money on objectives that are the constitutional concerns of the states. They also come freighted with detailed federal directives that deprive state and local officials of the ability to meet their own responsibilities in their own ways and undermine their citizens' ability to ensure that their taxes will be used to meet local priorities rather than those of distant bureaucracies.

Congress's infatuation with grants programs has its source in a series of Supreme Court cases dealing with the Constitution's Spending Clause, which authorizes the federal government to collect taxes with which "to pay the Debts and provide for the common Defense and general Welfare of the United States." The Court has construed the general welfare language as allowing Congress to "induce" states to accept federal directives regarding matters that fall within the states' exclusive constitutional authority and that Congress itself has no power to regulate. The inducing takes the form of offers of federal subsidies for a vast range of state activities. If a state accepts the offer, it is bound by the regulations that come with the money. The states are free to decline the subsidies, but experience has demonstrated that "free" money is extraordinarily hard to refuse, however onerous the attached conditions.

As I will demonstrate at some length in my chapter on costs, those conditions can be onerous indeed, but they are by no means the only burdens that attend the acceptance of federal funds. To cite just a few, grants-in-aid programs add a costly layer of administrative expense at the federal level as well as increasing administrative costs to the states. The use of federal money triggers a host of mandates (such as the obligation to pay union wage scales on construction work financed with federal dollars) that can add substantially to what a state would spend on a particular project if it were only using its own money. Uniform federal rules deny states the ability to respond to local conditions as they would if free to handle the work their own way, and to the degree that state officials serve as implementers of federal policies, their citizens are effectively disenfranchised. They no longer have a voice in the design and management of projects that can have the greatest impact on their lives. And the proliferation of grants programs imposes major costs on Congress itself.

Senators and representatives are public servants, but they

are also human beings who are subject to the ambitions and temptations that are part of our nature. They have discovered that the Court's construction of the Spending Clause provides them with the easiest way to ingratiate themselves to constituents and ensure their own reelection. They can now focus on their constituents' most immediate concerns which, in the nature of things, will involve such parochial matters as the condition of local roads, the education of their children, and the safety of their communities—matters that are the immediate responsibility of their state or local officials. And so they respond to those concerns by introducing legislation that will authorize transfers of federal money to the local highway commission or school or fire department—subject, of course, to regulations that Congress itself has no direct power to impose. Creating grants is not only politically rewarding; it is safe. Few will object to a proposal for such motherhood issues as care for the homeless or better nutrition for kids. But any politician intrepid enough to propose a one-dollar reduction in Medicare payments in order to avert the program's bankruptcy will have AARP's 40,000,000 members calling for his scalp.

To cite an example of Spending Clause incentives at work, within weeks of his election, my newest senator (and former congressman) began taking one-hour weekend bus trips in his state so that he might strike up conversations with ordinary citizens in what he referred to as an "informal environment." According to the newspaper story reporting on one of those trips, his fellow riders expressed concerns over low wages (he advised his listeners that he favored raising the federal minimum wage to $10, one dollar more than the scheduled Connecticut minimum), the difficulties of finding jobs, the high cost of education, and the need for more affordable housing— the same concerns they would have expressed had they been in a conversation with their governor or mayor. One woman informed him that she depended for a third of her income on a bus that operated until midnight thanks to a federal grant that would soon expire. The senator assured her that he favored its continuance. As he told the reporter, "I heard loud and clear how significant extended bus hours are," and on his return to Washington I have no doubt that he did his best to ensure that the federal grant would be renewed. Apparently none of the riders raised questions about the Middle East, or immigration law, or Medicare reform, or other issues that only a federal senator could deal with.

From my senator's perspective, this was an enormously productive trip. That one-hour bus ride earned him a favorable newspaper story and will consolidate a reputation for ministering to his constituents' concerns. As one of them remarked, "He could be at home relaxing. Instead he's on a bus trip with us." Of course, he might also have spent the time studying what he and his colleagues might do to address a host of problems that lie beyond the power of governors and mayors and that only Congress can address. I am not criticizing my senator. He is merely playing the current congressional game, and doing so with energy and imagination. My problem is with the game itself.

If I had been on that bus, I would have expressed a very different set of concerns, not because I was any wiser than my fellow citizens but because over the past forty-four years my work has immersed me in questions of national policy that only members of Congress can address. Had my senator asked me, I would have told him that my greatest worry was over the future the little girl seated across the aisle from us will face if Congress fails to screw up the courage to address our deficits and the runaway costs of our entitlement programs. In time she and her playmates will be faced with economy-crushing levels of taxation and/or savings-destroying rates of inflation if Congress fails to act. That is the sort of problem my senator and his colleagues in Washington should be concentrating on, not matters like bus schedules that governors and mayors are far better able to address.

This is not to disparage a U.S. senator's interest in municipal bus schedules, but the brutal fact is that we face a host of critical problems that only Congress can address. For years, both sides of the congressional aisles have known that the trajectory of entitlement spending will soon reach a point where we will be unable to honor promises made to the elderly, a trajectory that left unchanged will soon reach unsustainable levels. They know that within fifteen years the Medicare trust fund will be exhausted and that within another three the Social Security fund will be as well. Yet nothing has been done to adjust programs designed fifty and eighty years ago, respectively, to meet twenty-first-century demographic realities. There is a broad agreement that our corporate tax rates need to be reduced if our businesses are to remain competitive in a global economy and that this can be done without a loss of revenue by weeding out the favors to special business and other interests that litter our tax codes. Although individual members of Congress have developed practical approaches to both entitlement and tax reforms, nothing happens. Administrative agencies run out of control, but congressional oversight committees seem unable to rein them in.

Congress's current dysfunction is rooted in its assumption, over the years, of more responsibilities than it can handle. As a result, its members now live a treadmill existence that no longer allows them time to study, learn, and think things through. Instead, they substitute political reflex for thought. To compound the problem, their eyes are now so fixed on their particular political bases that they hesitate to make the compromises that the legislative process requires, and to ensure reelection, they avoid coming to grips with divisive issues whenever they can. When members of Congress do manage to enact a complex piece of legislation, they no longer have the time or patience to attend to all the minutiae that responsible legislation requires. Instead, they pass the messy details along to federal agencies, which spin out the regulations that will give the law shape. So no one, including those who drafted those laws, really knows how their handiwork will affect the real world until the regulations have been issued and put into effect.

In sum, the American Republic is in a very bad way today. It is spending itself into bankruptcy and its legislative branch appears institutionally incapable of focusing on critical problems long enough to resolve them. The purpose of this book is to propose a *single*, easily understood way of addressing both of these problems, one that should appeal to Americans across the ideological spectrum. In crafting it, I have drawn on my experience as a United States senator who has some knowledge of the temptations faced by elected officials, and as a federal appellate judge who has had to deal with the costly litigation that opaque regulations can generate. If adopted, my reform will result in a major reduction in federal spending while freeing Congress to focus on the critical national issues that are its unique responsibility. As radical as it may at first appear, my modest proposal, namely the eradication of all federal grants to state and local governments, requires no more than that members of Congress honor the principle of federalism that is embedded in the Constitution they are pledged to defend.

As a return to federalism is at the heart of my proposed reform, I will begin with a reminder of its roots and logic.

SAVING
CONGRESS
FROM ITSELF

★ 1 ★

THE CONSTITUTION'S ORIGINAL DESIGN

. . . AND ITS EROSION

THE ORIGINAL UNDERSTANDING

American independence was won and the Republic created by a remarkable generation of men who turned a rebellion against the British crown into a transforming moment in human history, one based on the revolutionary proposition that all men are created equal and are endowed by their Creator with fundamental rights that no government has the moral authority to set aside. But in attaining independence, the Founders were faced with the formidable task of creating a government that could operate effectively while protecting the liberties for which the Revolution had been fought.

In *Federalist* No. 51, James Madison described that challenge as follows: "In framing a government which is to be administered by men over men, the great difficulty lies in this: you must first enable the government to control the governed; and in the next place oblige it to control itself." He also noted that while a "dependence on the people is, no doubt, the primary control on the government; . . . experience has taught mankind the necessity of auxiliary precautions."

The Founders had no illusions about human nature. They understood that the drive to accumulate power, whether by an individual despot or a parliamentary majority, was the historic enemy of individual freedom. They therefore incorporated two "precautions" into the Constitution: its system of separation of powers, with its checks and balances, and the principle of federalism. In describing the latter, Madison explained:

> The powers delegated by the proposed Constitution to the federal government are few and defined. . . . The powers reserved to the several States will extend to all the objects which, in the ordinary course of affairs, concern the lives, liberties, and properties of the people, and the internal order, improvement, and prosperity of the State. *[Federalist No. 45]*

During the debates over the Constitution's ratification, many expressed a concern that this allocation of responsibilities was not clear enough in the document itself. As a consequence, the first Congress made it explicit in the Tenth Amendment of the Bill of Rights, which provides that "[t]he powers not delegated to the United States by the Constitution, nor prohibited by it to the States, are reserved to the States respectively, or to the people."

The powers delegated to Congress are identified in Section 8 of Article I of the Constitution. Section 8 consists of a series of clauses identifying the grants of legislative authority that the members of the Constitutional Convention concluded were necessary to ensure the success of their new nation, such as the authority to tax and borrow, regulate foreign and interstate commerce, establish post offices, maintain military forces, provide copyright and patent protection, and exercise a half dozen other powers. Those grants are referred to as the "enumerated powers." Implicit in this arrangement was the understanding that those not enumerated were reserved to the states or the people themselves, an understanding made explicit in the Tenth Amendment.

That reservation was critical to the Constitution's design. The central government it created had no powers other than those specifically assigned to it by the people in their state-by-state ratifying conventions. It also explains why the Constitution's framers saw no reason to include guarantees of the freedom of religion and speech and the other protections against governmental abuse found in the Bill of Rights that the first Congress adopted. As one of the Constitution's principal authors, James Wilson, explained in response to objections that it did not contain a bill of rights:

> There are two kinds of government; that where general power is intended to be given to the legislature and that where the powers are particularly enumerated. In the last case, the implied result is, that nothing more is intended to be given, than what is so enumerated. . . . On the other hand, when general legislative powers are given, then the people part with their authority, and . . . retain nothing. But in a government like the proposed one, there can be no necessity for a bill of rights. For . . . the people never part with their power. *[Speech to the Pennsylvania Ratifying Convention, December 4, 1787]*

As the people had not granted the new government the power to enact laws relating to religion, speech, etc., there was no occasion to include protections against the abuse of powers that hadn't been granted.

It is important to make this point about the Bill of Rights because so many Americans today do not understand that the structure of the Constitution itself is the guarantor of their freedoms rather than the Bill of Rights. The American Civil Liberties Union's website, for example, contains the following statement: "The Constitution was remarkable, but deeply flawed. For one thing, it did not include a specific declaration—

or bill—of individual rights. It specified what the government could do but did not say what it could not do." The answer, of course, is that the government had no authority to do anything other than what the Constitution specified it could do. Those who insisted on the adoption of the Bill of Rights, however, have been vindicated over the years, because experience has shown that the drive for power has a way of undermining the most carefully designed restraints. It is, nevertheless, a guarantee of only a handful of specific rights, however important.

The broader protection is to be found in the Tenth Amendment's explicit statement that all authority not granted to the federal government belongs to the states or to the people. As Madison explained in *Federalist* No. 51, the tensions between the state and federal governments would safeguard our liberties: "In the compound republic of America, the power surrendered by the people is first divided between two distinct governments. . . . Hence a double security arises to the rights of the people. The different governments will control each other, at the same time that each will be controlled by itself [a reference to the separation of powers and checks and balances that exist within each level of government]."

It is worth noting that the Constitution's allocation of responsibilities between two levels of government conforms with the venerable "Rule of Subsidiarity," one that was adopted in the 1992 Treaty of Maastricht as a central constitutional principle of the European Union, however ignored in practice. It recognizes a hierarchy of responsibilities beginning with those of the individual. Under that principle, you and I are primarily responsible for managing our own lives and caring for our families, while governmental responsibilities are allocated to the lowest levels able to exercise them. Its effect is to decentralize political power and ensure, wherever feasible, that officials who are the closest to ordinary citizens and most familiar with the relevant facts will be responsible for making decisions most immediately affecting them. One significant benefit of this arrangement is that it permits states and local communities to serve as laboratories for the development of a variety of approaches to shared problems.

Those were the virtues of the federalism that its framers built into our Constitution. They consciously limited the federal government's authority to the handful of responsibilities they thought necessary to enable their new nation to function effectively; and with the enactment of the Tenth Amendment, they explicitly preserved the states' exclusive authority over all other proper governmental concerns. That, at least, was their intention.

FEDERALISM'S EMASCULATION

Unfortunately, those who insisted on the enactment of the Tenth Amendment have proven prescient. Over the years, successive Congresses and an accommodating Supreme Court have emasculated federalism to the point where there is virtually no exercise of federal power that the Court will deem unconstitutional. This has been accomplished largely through constructions of the Constitution's Interstate Commerce and Spending Clauses. My concern here is with the latter, which, in relevant part, empowers Congress to collect taxes and other revenues "to pay the Debts and provide for the common Defence and general Welfare of the United States." The mischief lies in the words "general Welfare."

During much of our history, the prevailing view was that that phrase did no more than place a limit on Congress's authority to spend by requiring that federal expenditures serve national as opposed to state or local purposes. Beginning with the 1937 case of *Steward Machine Co. v. Davis*, however, the Supreme Court has held that in its pursuit of the general welfare, Congress is authorized to provide states with funds to implement programs that Congress itself has no power to write into law. In 1987, in *South Dakota v. Dole*, the Court declared that the deference it owed Congress was such that it is "question[able] whether 'general welfare' is a judicially enforceable restriction at all." Thus in pursuit of its unchallengeable understanding of what constitutes the public good, Congress is now empowered to use federal funds to "induce the States to adopt policies that the Federal Government itself could not impose," to quote Chief Justice Roberts' majority opinion in the case that found the Affordable Care Act, or Obamacare, to be constitutional. This is the source of Congress's authority to enact most of the grants-in-aid programs now in effect.

In sum, although ours is understood to be a government of limited powers, the Supreme Court has construed one of those powers as providing Congress with the ability to bribe the states to adopt policies that lie beyond its own constitutional authority to prescribe—a position that caused Justice Sandra Day O'Connor to declare, in her *South Dakota v. Dole* dissent: "If the spending power is to be limited only by Congress' notion of the general welfare, the reality . . . is that the Spending Clause gives power to the Congress . . . to become a parliament of the whole people, subject to no restrictions save such as are self-imposed. This was not the Framers' plan and it is not the meaning of the Spending Clause." So much for James Madison's description of the federal government's powers as "few and defined."

Congress' ability to bribe is not absolute, however. As the Court held in the Obamacare case, the law's requirement that states expand their Medicaid programs was unconstitutional because the penalty for their failure to do so was so severe (the forfeiture of existing federal Medicaid contributions) that the states would be coerced into compliance despite their sovereign right to decline. The Court, however, finds no objection to noncoercive offers of federal money that are so economically or politically irresistible that a state has little real-life alternative but to accept them along with conditions that Congress has no independent authority to impose on them.

It is beyond dispute that these developments have effectively abolished the division of governmental labors that the founding generation felt was so important to the success of their new nation. Times have changed dramatically over the past two centuries, however, so the question today is whether we are better off as a result of this expansion of the federal government's role in American life. In addressing that question, this book will deal only with the costs and effects of the federal grants-in-aid programs that offer states and communities various sums on the condition that the funds be used to implement policies designed in Washington. Thus my references to "federal grants" or "grants-in-aid programs" are limited to those offered to states and localities as opposed, for example, to a grant to a state university in support of medical research; and when I refer to "states" as grantees, that word should be understood to include their subdivisions as well.

What is important to keep in mind is that the states are free to decline to participate in grants-in-aid programs. That represents a recognition by Congress that the programs deal with responsibilities that lie within the states' competence. That in turn raises questions over the practical merits (the constitutional niceties aside) of Congress's involvement in areas that lie beyond those assigned to it by the Constitution.

★ 2 ★

THE GRANTS-IN-AID CORNUCOPIA

THE HISTORY AND NATURE OF GRANTS-IN-AID

I became aware of the imaginative scope of federal grants programs when, on my retirement, I moved to a small community in northwest Connecticut and subscribed to a daily paper published in a nearby city. I soon found it filled with reports of federal grants in support of an astonishing variety of civic purposes. To cite just a few, they included financing for an art center honoring Katharine Hepburn, the grant of $1.5 million of federal highway trust funds to restore a vandalized train station that had long since been converted to nontransportation uses, funds for the purchase of a farm's development rights in order to preserve a town's rural character, money for the beautification of roads leading into a small industrial town, payment of eighty percent of the cost of replacing a one-lane bridge connecting two small communities a dozen miles from my home, and a grant for widening of sidewalks bordering two streets leading to a local school.

That last is my favorite example of congressional imagination. Those sidewalks in Plymouth, Connecticut (population 12,000) were to be widened with the help of a $430,000 grant from the Federal Safe Routes to School Program whose stated purpose, quite literally, was to fight obesity by encouraging children to walk or bicycle to school. To that end, in 2005, Congress created the five-year program and financed it with $612 million of federal highway trust funds. If Plymouth parents had been offered that money to help battle their children's obesity, it is anything but obvious that broadening sidewalks would have been their weapon of choice. But that is beside the point. Congress created the fund and no one turns down money from Washington, not even Connecticut taxpayers who send $1.45 to Washington for every dollar they get back in federal grants. They accept the money because they know that those recycled dollars will otherwise be spent widening sidewalks in another state.

Lest anyone conclude that these quixotic examples are peculiar to Connecticut, herewith are some others gleaned from Senator Tom Coburn's 2013 "Wastebook," in which he reported particularly egregious examples of government waste:

- $50 million for a Maryland "transit center" that had quintupled in cost;

- $65 million to enable New York and New Jersey to advertise that they are good places for business (never mind the truth-in-advertising concerns);

- $195,000 for a substance-abuse program's Hollywood party;

- $3.9 million on an airport in St. Cloud, Minnesota, which has no daily commercial flights;

- $1.25 million for the State of Florida to settle a lawsuit brought by one of its contractors;

- $30 million for "coastal conservation" in Mississippi, part of which was spent on an art museum;

- $800,000 for Las Vegas to award a prize to someone who had a good economic development idea;

- $368,000 of "community development" money that went to a Montana electric golf cart maker; and

- $532,000 to beautify one block on main street in Rossville, Kansas (pop. 1,150).

It is easy to poke fun at such federal expenditures because it is hard to think of purposes more quintessentially local in nature or further removed from the pressing concerns that ought to command Congress's attention. The vast majority of federal grants, however, deal with needs that are generally accepted as important, such as the construction and maintenance of roads, assistance for the poor, and education. But others, such as the one that would widen sidewalks to fight juvenile obesity, illustrate Congress's incurable temptation to propose a federal solution to any problem or need, however parochial.

That temptation is as old as the Republic. Thomas Jefferson, who vigorously opposed expansions of federal power proposed by Alexander Hamilton, nevertheless approved federal aid for the construction of what came to be known as the Cumberland Road. Its purpose was to serve newly settled areas beyond the Appalachians. James Monroe, however, later vetoed a bill for its preservation and repair based on his understanding that Congress's spending authority was restricted "to purposes of common defense and of general, not local, national, not State, benefit" (message to Congress, May 4, 1822). While other early Congresses occasionally enacted legislation providing for the construction of roads and canals, until the outbreak of the Civil War, such proposals were routinely vetoed as unconstitutional.

The first grant-in-aid program of the modern kind was the Morrill Act of 1862. It authorized grants of federal lands to the states on the condition that they or the funds derived from their sale be used by the states for the establishment of agricultural colleges. President Buchanan vetoed an earlier version as unconstitutional, but the 1862 Act included a provision for military training in the colleges' curricula that may have eased its acceptance as the Civil War was then in its second year.

Almost a century later, the federal government became involved in education in a significant way with the enactment of the National Defense Education Act of 1958. That was Washington's response to the Soviet Union's launching of Sputnik, the first satellite to achieve orbit, and the resulting fear that the United States was falling behind the Soviets in the field of science. Accordingly, because of what was viewed as a threat to national security, Congress authorized the distribution of grants to schools at all levels to accelerate our training of mathematicians and scientists. From that point on, the defense rationale was abandoned and Washington's involvement in education grew at such a rate that twenty-one years later, in 1979, Congress found it necessary to create a Department of Education and a cabinet secretary to oversee it.

That same concern for national security launched the federal government's wholesale involvement in the construction of highways. The need to facilitate the movement of troops and supplies in a national emergency was the justification given for President Dwight Eisenhower's National Interstate and Defense Highway Act of 1956, which paid ninety percent of the cost of building a 41,000-mile interstate highway system. That ambitious project was financed by federal taxes on gasoline paid into the Highway Trust Fund. Because of its military rationale, this legislation clearly fell within the scope of the Constitution's Defense Clause. Over the years, however, that fund has increasingly been used for a broad range of purely local uses, such as the replacement of a one-lane bridge linking two small Connecticut communities.

It was not until Lyndon Johnson's Great Society that the creation of grants-in-aid programs became epidemic. In 1960, there were 132 of them; but by 1970, their number had quadrupled to 530. Over those ten years, transfers to the states rose from 7.6 percent of federal outlays to 12.3 percent (see Chris Edwards, *Policy Analysis*, no. 593). By then, the proliferation of federal urban grants led Peter Drucker to note, in his essay "The Sickness of Government," that

during the past three decades, federal payments to the big cities have increased almost a hundred-fold for all kinds of programs, whereas results from this incredible dollar-flood are singularly unimpressive. What *is* impressive is the administrative incompetence. We now have ten times as many government agencies concerned with city problems as we had in 1939. We have increased by a factor of a thousand or so the number of reports and papers that have to be filled out before anything can be done in the city. Social workers in New York City spend some 70 or 80 per cent of their time filling out papers for Washington, for the state government in Albany, and for New York City. No more than 20 or 30 per cent of their time, that is, almost an hour and a half a day, is available for their clients, the poor. As James Reston reported in *The New York Times* (November 23, 1966), there were then 170 different federal aid programs on the books, financed by over 400 separate appropriations and administered by 21 federal departments and agencies aided by 150 Washington bureaus and over 400 regional offices. One Congressional session alone passed 20 health programs, 17 new educational programs, 15 new economic development programs, 12 new programs for the cities, 17 new resources development programs, and 4 new manpower training programs, each with its own administrative machinery.

But that was just the beginning. Congress had become so addicted to this form of federal largesse that by 2010 the number of grants programs available to states and/or localities exceeded 1,100 and, at a cost of $608.4 billion, they constituted 17 percent of the federal budget for that year, its third largest category of expenditures after entitlements and defense. They

TRENDS IN FEDERAL GRANTS
TO STATE AND LOCAL GOVERNMENTS

Distributions by function. Outlays in billions of dollars.

	1970	1980	1990	2000	2010	2015 *(est.)*
Natural resources and environment	0.4	5.4	3.7	4.5	9.1	6.5
Agriculture	0.6	0.6	1.3	0.7	0.8	1.0
Transportation	4.6	13.0	19.2	32.2	61.0	67.2
Community and regional development	1.8	6.5	5.0	8.7	18.8	17.4
Education, training, employment, and social services	6.4	21.9	21.8	36.7	97.6	69.3
Health	3.8	15.8	43.9	124.8	290.2	357.0
Income security	5.8	18.5	36.8	68.7	115.2	190.1
Administration of justice	0.0	0.5	0.6	5.3	5.1	4.7
General government	0.5	8.6	2.3	2.1	5.2	4.1
Other	0.1	0.7	0.8	2.1	5.4	4.4
Total	24.1	91.4	135.3	285.9	608.4	640.8

SOURCE: Budget of the U.S. Government, Fiscal Year 2015, Historical Tables.
NOTE: Rounded numbers not reflected in totals.

now provide states with about a quarter of their revenues. The adjacent table underscores the relentless increase in federal grants, which are projected to expand to $643.3 billion in 2014.

It is clear that over the past two generations we have experienced a radical change in how we govern ourselves.

ARGUMENTS IN SUPPORT OF FEDERAL GRANTS

There are essentially four arguments in favor of the federal grants programs. First, the federal government is better able to enlist the expertise required to craft the most effective approaches to the problems that the states share; second, it is in the best position to mobilize the money required to implement them; third, the states remain free to decline federal assistance and thus preserve their autonomy; and fourth, the grants provide a mechanism for the redistribution of money from wealthy states to the poorer ones, thus making it easier for the latter to maintain the educational and other standards to which all Americans are entitled. Each of those arguments has its limitations.

It is true that Washington is far better able than the states to call on the best academic and professional talent in designing programs. But that argument begs the question of whether any body of experts, however wise, will be able to come up with a single best approach to the provision of a social safety net or education or a host of other government services in a country as large and diverse as ours. Nor is it clear that the solutions academics produce on paper will work as expected when put into practice. The fact is that there is no evidence that federally mandated standards have ensured better results than those the states have fashioned on their own; and, as will be demonstrated in my discussion of costs, those standards can prove very expensive.

Take education as an example. As the quality of our public

schools is of particular importance, it is worth noting that Washington's first significant involvement in education began almost fifty years ago with the enactment of the Elementary and Secondary Education Act of 1965. Yet as Andrew Coulson has demonstrated in his exhaustive 2014 study, "State Education Trends," during the succeeding decades there has been no improvement in the quality of education nationally "despite the near tripling of the inflation-adjusted cost of putting a child through the K-12 system." In the one jurisdiction for which the federal government has constitutional responsibility, namely the District of Columbia, it has been abysmal. In recent years, the federal government has focused on raising standards though President George W. Bush's "No Child Left Behind" program and President Obama's "Race to the Top" with, at best, mixed results to date. As I will demonstrate later, however, federal educational initiatives have placed extraordinary burdens on the states.

With respect to the second argument, it is also true that it is far easier for Washington to raise money, whether through taxes or borrowing. States are required to balance their books and their ability to borrow is restricted. Those restrictions impose a discipline on the states that is not to be found in Washington because the federal government has a virtually unlimited ability to borrow. Its debt, however, is rising at an alarming rate and, in time, that debt will have to be repaid. What must be stressed is that the money that flows into Washington comes either from taxes paid by residents of the states or from loans that will have to be repaid by their children or grandchildren. The ease with which Washington can borrow is not an advantage; it is a growing problem.

The third argument is true as far as it goes. States are indeed free to decline participation in federal grants programs. The reality is that in only the rarest cases are they able to resist the offer of money from the federal government. I recall the testimony of a southern governor who appeared as a witness at one of my Senate Public Works Committee hearings. He described the punishing political flak he had endured when he had the temerity to decline forty percent federal funding for an urgently needed state highway project. He had declined it because abiding by the federal rule book would have delayed the project's completion by three years and required compliance with standards more appropriate for Alaska than his state. Adherence to the standards would have increased the project's cost to such a degree that the governor was able to save money and a substantial amount of time by forgoing the federal grant. The irresistible political pressure produced by the offer of federal money was neatly captured in a March 3, 1971, *Wall Street Journal* editorial by Robert L. Bartley that discussed the "gold-plated octagon problem" lamented by officials in Washington. Their thesis was that if Congress were to enact a law offering to reimburse half the cost of erecting gold-plated octagons, every town in America would soon have one.

I acknowledge, however, that Obamacare's attempt to achieve a major increase in Medicaid enrollment has met with unprecedented resistance despite its provision for one hundred percent federal financing during the program's first three years. As of August 2014, twenty-one states have declined this offer because, over the years, federal prodding and inducements had already caused Medicaid to become the largest expense on state budgets. In recent years, there has been increasing question as to whether the accompanying federal rules permit the most effective ways of ensuring adequate health care for the poor. There is also concern that Obamacare's raising of the eligibility level to 138 percent of the Federal poverty line, in combination with other welfare measures that are devoid of work requirements, will create disincentives to securing employment that could lead to permanent dependency. As a number of governors have pointed out, work requirements were the key to the 1998 welfare reform's success in reducing welfare rolls and putting people back to work. In the view of those governors, the acceptance of even one hundred percent federal financing during the initial years would have locked their states into a set of federal eligibility standards and regulations that would cripple their ability to achieve necessary reforms. Those considerations explain this atypical refusal to take the federal bait.

With respect to the fourth defense of grants-in-aid, it is true that the programs effect a significant transfer of money from the have to the have-not states. In 2005, for example, Connecticut received 69 cents in grants for every dollar it sent to Washington. By contrast, New Mexico received $2.03. Thirty-two states are net beneficiaries of this redistribution and that, in turn, provides their representatives in Congress with a special incentive to support those programs. There are, of course, some strong arguments in favor of this redistribution: the have-not states may not be able to afford the quality of services, such as education, that the richer ones can provide. As I will explain later, however, if federal transfers from the haves to the have-nots are indeed justified, there is a more effective way of accomplishing that goal without saddling the recipients, rich and poor alike, with tangles of federal regulations.

★ 3 ★

THE PROGRAMS' COSTS

COSTS TO THE FEDERAL TREASURY

The cost of the grants programs to the federal government is considerably larger than just the number of dollars transferred to the states. They include the expenses incurred by the various agencies that are charged with the programs' administration as well as the extra costs incurred as a result of Congress's habit of creating a host of overlapping programs that address essentially the same objectives.

COSTS OF ADMINISTRATION

In 2010, a total of $608.4 billion was appropriated for the programs that are the subject of this book. A Congressional Research Service report, "Federal Grants-in-Aid Administration: A Primer," describes what is involved in administering them. What it calls their "life cycle" begins with a pre-award stage and then proceeds through grant award, grant program administration, and post-award audit stages. Each involves detailed work in establishing the ground rules for awarding grants, the processing of grant applications, the negotiation of agreements with successful applicants governing the use of their grants, oversight of the grantee's compliance with its obligations, and a final audit after the work financed by a grant has been completed.

As the CRS report notes, "[g]enerally, federal agencies separate grant management functions into three categories: financial management, program administration, and grant oversight," which are assigned to separate agency divisions manned by grant specialists. Needless to say, all of this requires a great deal of money, but there is little data available to indicate how much. To give some idea of their extent, however, in 1978 the Government Accounting Office reported that those costs ranged from 0.3 to 28.5 percent of what was transferred to the states, and it later reported that the administration of the $290 million Sports Fishing Restoration Program cost $22 million. The Cato Institute's February 2011 *Tax & Budget Bulletin* 63, "Federal Aid-to-State Programs Top 1,100," estimated that the federal agencies in charge of the grants "consume roughly 10 percent of the value of the aid in administration." If accurate, that means that the federal cost of managing the 2010 grants came to approximately $61 billion.

COSTS OF PROGRAM REDUNDANCY

At the request of Congress, in 2011 the Government Accountability Office issued a report that is charitably titled *Opportunities to Reduce Potential Duplication in Government Programs, Save Tax Dollars, and Enhance Revenue*. I say "charitably" because there is nothing potential about the duplications it identifies in virtually every area where Congress has attempted to solve state and local problems through the issuance of regulation-ridden federal handouts.

The report cites more than one hundred programs dealing

with surface transportation, eighty with economic development, eighty-two with teacher training, forty-seven with job training, twenty with various aspects of homelessness, eighteen with food assistance for the poor, and the list goes on, as do the headaches and expense of sorting them all out. (A sampling of these redundancies will be found in Appendix A.) The online description of the GAO report summarized its findings as follows:

> Overlap and fragmentation among government programs or activities can be the harbingers of unnecessary duplication. In this report we include 81 areas for consideration drawn from the GAO's prior and ongoing work. We present 34 areas where agencies, offices, or initiatives have similar or overlapping objectives or provide similar services to the same populations; or where government missions are fragmented across multiple agencies or programs. We also present 47 additional areas—beyond those directly related to duplication, overlap, or fragmentation—describing other opportunities for agencies or Congress to consider taking action that could either reduce the cost of government operations or enhance revenue collections for the Treasury. All of these areas span a range of agencies and government missions: agriculture, defense, economic development, energy, general government, health, homeland security international affairs, and social services. Collectively, by reducing or eliminating duplication, overlap, or fragmentation and addressing these other cost savings opportunities, the federal government could potentially save billions of tax dollars annually and help agencies provide more efficient and effective services—but these actions will require some difficult decisions.

Decisions that, to date, Congress has found it too difficult to make.

Congress's habit of enacting multiple programs for achieving one objective has proven both aggravating and counterproductive. The forty-seven programs designed to put people back to work were entrusted to the Departments of Labor,

Education, and Health and Human Services, but while those departments have made an effort to resolve some of the problems resulting from the programmatic overlaps, a House committee staff report noted that "an obstacle to further progress in achieving greater administrative efficiencies is that little information is available about the strategies and results of such initiatives" (cited in the GAO report). That is a polite way of saying that although those programs authorize the expenditure of $18 billion, no one knows whether they are helping people find jobs. In commenting on the GAO's statement that "little is known about the effectiveness" of the forty-seven programs, Gregory Korte observed that little was known "because half haven't had a performance review since 2004 and only five have ever had a study to determine whether job seekers in the program do better than those who don't participate" (*USA Today*, February 2, 2011).

The GAO also reported that three different federal departments, as well as numerous state and local agencies, are involved in administering the eighteen programs that have the common objective of ensuring that the minimum nutrition needs of the poor are met. But again, the different standards and qualifications imbedded in the laws result in overlaps and inconsistent requirements that preclude a comprehensive approach to an important human need. Then there are the twenty programs that, in 2009, authorized the expenditure of $2.9 billion to meet the needs of the homeless. Thanks again to conflicting legislative marching orders, the various federal agencies charged with providing for those needs have found it impossible to come up with an efficient, coordinated approach. According to the GAO, the lack of federal coordination was viewed by a number of local agencies "as an important barrier to the effective delivery of services" to the homeless.

And so it goes. In area after area, policy analysts have identified important efficiencies and savings that could be achieved with the elimination of the redundancies and fragmentation that characterize so many categories of grants. The GAO has been calling attention to these problems since the 1990s, but Congress can't seem to focus the attention required to address them. "Federal Grants-in-Aid Administration: A Primer" says it all:

> The growing number, perceived fragmentaticn, and complexity of these programs create challenges for federal agencies interested in standardizing various financial and administrative aspects of grant program management. . . . This variation in federal grant administration makes it difficult for Congress to compare program performance, both within and among federal agencies, and to exercise its oversight of federal agencies.

There are two reasons why this should be so. Overlapping programs may fall within the jurisdiction of different congressional committees. That can make it more difficult for any one of them to grasp the problems that the Congressional Research Service describes. There is also the problem of human nature. Committees are reluctant to cede jurisdiction over particular concerns, especially those with political sex appeal. Therefore, the consolidation of programs that fall within the jurisdiction of several committees is apt to face resistance because it will require that one or more committees bow out of the field.

COSTS TO THE STATES

The costs to the states of grant-in-aid programs take a number of forms—some of them obvious, others not, and all difficult to quantify. They are, however, significant. As I review the many ways the grants programs impose costs on the states beyond the states' shares of the cost of federally subsidized projects, I acknowledge my indebtedness to Mr. Chris Edwards, of the Cato Institute, who has published a series of studies documenting the distortions triggered by the availability of manna from Washington.

GRANT APPLICATIONS AND COMPLIANCE

Most federal transfers to the states take the form of either "formula" or discretionary "projects" grants. The former are the fewest in number but deliver the largest sums of money. Medicaid, the formula health program for the poor, is the biggest of them all, with grants to the states totaling $250 billion in 2012 (2014 White House Office of Management and Budget's Historical Tables). The laws authorizing formula grants determine how much each state receives based on such factors as population and wealth, with recipient states being required to contribute various percentages of the programs' costs. The administrative expenses incurred in those cases are relatively light.

The situation is dramatically different when it comes to projects grants because their allocation is discretionary. In those cases, the states and their subdivisions must compete for shares of the available funds and each program is subject to its own bewildering set of rules. Applicants must prepare grant applications that describe in great detail the projects for which funding is requested. If their applications are granted, they must then negotiate grant agreements, conduct environmental impact and historic preservation reviews where required, and prepare periodic performance and financial reports as the work progresses. All of this involves the expenditure of significant sums over and above what it would have cost the states to conduct the identical projects if they didn't have to comply with the rules imposed by Washington.

UNFUNDED MANDATES

Another element of cost consists of unfunded federal mandates. Some of those are imposed by the rules that accompany the grants themselves while others are to be found in independent legislation such as the Davis-Bacon Act of 1931. That law requires that "locally prevailing wages" be paid for all work funded in whole or part by the federal government, such as housing and highway construction. As Philip K. Howard explained in his book *The Rule of Nobody: Saving America from Dead Laws and Broken Government*, the Davis-Bacon requirement is "basically a union perk that costs taxpayers about 20 percent more than actual labor rates. This requirement comes with a mass of red tape; bureaucrats in the Labor Department must set wages, as a matter of law, for each category of construction worker in each of three thousand counties in America" (quoted in the *Wall Street Journal*, March 25, 2014). Aside from running up administrative costs, the law's effect is to deny federal grant recipients the substantial savings that might be achieved in competitive bidding that is open to nonunion contractors. Other examples are the Accommodations for People with Handicaps and Individuals with Disabilities Education Acts. Both laws have admirable objectives, but they are individually complex (application of the latter requires mastering 1,700 pages of regulations) and impose very large costs in order to achieve objectives that the states are in a far better position to address than distant bureaucrats.

A February 2006 report by the Fairfax County, Virginia, County Executive to his Board of Supervisors gives some idea of the federal mandates' impact on state and local governments. He estimated that in 2006 those mandates would cost Fairfax County approximately $423 million toward which the federal government would be contributing around $140 million, leaving a balance of $283 million to be met by the county, the state, and various users' fees. Neither the county nor the state had any say in the design of those mandates, but they were stuck with the bill. Furthermore, while laws creating federal mandates may contain provisions for grants to help pay for them, there is no guarantee that Congress will get around to appropriating the necessary funds.

When combined with a tangle of regulations, the burden imposed by mandates can be particularly aggravating. In Diane Ravitch's 1999 study on "The National Agenda in Elementary and Secondary Education," found in *Setting National Priorities: The 2000 Election and Beyond*, for example, one Florida official is quoted as saying that as a result of

> the crushing burden caused by too many federal regulations, procedures, and mandates, Florida spent millions of dollars every year to administer inflexible, categorical federal programs that divert precious dollars away from raising student achievement. . . . [T]here are 297 state employees to oversee and administer approximately $1 billion in federal funds. By contrast, we have 394 state-funded positions to oversee and administer approximately $7 billion in state funds. *[pp. 283–84]*

Education programs have proven so complex that they have sparked new fields of litigation. The National Head Start Association has formed its own Legal Advisory Service, and one expert cited by Ms. Ravitch called special education "a lawyer's playground" while another described it as "an empire controlled by lawyers, bureaucrats, and interests groups." (I had occasion to hear some of their cases as a judge.)

In 1984, the Advisory Commission on Intergovernmental Relations issued a report titled "Regulatory Federalism: Policy, Process, Impact, and Reform" in which it estimated that by 1980, independent and grant-associated mandates had reached a total of 1,259, of which 1,036 were grant related. In a subsequent report, the ACIR declared that those mandates

> had reached such proportions as to constitute an overextension of the constitutionally delegated powers of the Congress and Executive, an abridgement of the authority of the citizens in their

state and local communities to govern their own affairs, and an impairment of the ability of citizens to hold their elected officials accountable for the public costs of their decisions.

["Federal Regulation of State and Local Governments:
The Mixed Record of the 1980s," 1993]

Unfortunately, as that report also points out, the Supreme Court has stated in *South Dakota v. Dole* and other recent cases that the constitutionality of those intrusions on state and local authority are immune from judicial review. Thus, as a practical matter, only Congress can restore the restraints on federal authority so clearly intended by the Constitution's authors.

The complaints against runaway mandates did lead to the 1995 passage of the Unfunded Mandate Reform Act, but that resulted in only a temporary decline in their number. Within a decade, state budgets were once again being distorted by Congress's imposition of standards and obligations that it neglected to fund. According to the National Conference of State Legislatures, those shortfalls totaled $29 billion in 2004 and were scheduled to reach $34 billion in 2005 with consequences that Pennsylvania Representative David Steil describes as follows: "Even in good economic times, costs like these are insidious. They cause state and local officials to cut services and to steal funds from worthy state programs to pay for federal ones. In bad economic times, these mandates are intolerable" (Molly Stauffer and Carl Tubbesing, "The Mandate Monster," *State Legislatures*, May 1, 2004).

The NCSL's president, Utah Speaker Martin Stephens, goes to the heart of the problem: it is not Congress's failure to fund its mandates, it is their "corrosive effect on our federal system." As he explains, "Federal policy priorities supplant state priorities. Legislatures' spending options are handcuffed by federal decisions. In other words, officials furthest removed from the voters are making budget decisions for state legislators and city councilmen." Unfortunately, "that's not easy to explain when all the voter wants to know is why the library had to cut its hours" (Stauffer and Tubbesing, "Mandate Monster"). And that is at the root of the problem: local and state voters are no longer in control of too many local and state decisions, decisions that are made by Washington agencies that even members of Congress find hard to control.

DISTORTING STATE PRIORITIES

As anyone will discover on browsing through the 3,000-page, twelve-pound Catalog of Federal Domestic Assistance, its offerings can prove enormously seductive, and in ways that have little to do with meeting a state's priorities. Consider, for example, the remarkable feat of grantsmanship that has enabled Connecticut to proceed with a highly controversial 9.4-mile busway between New Britain and Hartford, cities that were already linked by bus service over an existing highway. In order to secure a total of $459.35 million in federal funding for the $572.69 million busway, the state was able to tap six different programs: the Section 5307 Urbanized Area Formula Funds ($18.2 million), Section 5309 Fixed Guideway Modernization Funds ($21.18 million), FHWA Flexible Funds ($112.75 million), FHWA NHS Funds ($6 million), Section 5309 Bus Discretionary ($25.92 million), and Section 5309 New Starts Share ($275.3 million). That last grant carried the day. As the *Hartford Courant* reported, "Monday's infusion of $275 million made Gov. Daniel P. Malloy's crucial support for the risky project awfully easy."

It was only when the federal grants reached 80.2 percent of the busway's projected cost that the state felt justified in committing the additional $113.34 million required to build it. But that meant that that money would not be available to meet the state's more pressing transportation needs, as described in an Associated Press story that appeared within a week of the time the bulldozers began clearing the ground for the busway.

According to that article, over two hundred of Connecticut's bridges were "fracture critical." That means that they failed to have the redundant protections required to protect them from collapse if a single vital component failed. Forty-nine of those bridges, with a daily traffic of 1.8 million vehicles, were also considered "structurally deficient." By contrast, the busway is projected to shorten the commute of an initial 13,400 commuters by a few minutes a day with a long-term projection of 16,300.

But priorities be damned. How can state officials be expected to resist the seductive offer of four federal dollars for every one of their own?

COST OF LOBBYING

Despite the costs and frustrations I have described, the lure of federal dollars remains so strong that states spend large amounts every year in support of organizations whose principal purpose is to lobby for categories of grants that meet parochial needs. For example, the Northeast-Midwest Institute, which represents eighteen states, works through formal coalitions of the region's congressional delegations to lobby representatives of other states to support programs of particular interest to the region. The National Association of State Departments of Agriculture's self-described purpose is "to influence the development and implementation of sound policy and programs at all levels of the federal government"; that is to say, sound policy as perceived by its constituents. States also rely on Washington lobbyists to help them milk the federal cow. According to the Sunlight Foundation, more than four hundred cities have also retained them, and their services are not cheap.

Then there are the private groups that are organized to ensure the flow of federal funds in support of particular causes, as exemplified by the National WIC (Women, Infants, and

Children) Association. Its purpose is to "promote quality nutrition services for all eligible mothers and young children." A glance at its 2013 legislative agenda makes it clear that it views the federal government as the appropriate source of all those services. Lobbying Washington, of course, requires far less effort than having to persuade each of the fifty states of the merits of the organization's proposals. There are a host of other such well-funded associations, all in the business of encouraging Congress to maintain or expand existing programs or to create new ones.

REDUCED ACCOUNTABILITY TO THE PEOPLE

One of the most insidious aspects of grants-in-aid programs is the diffusion of responsibility that makes them so attractive to federal and state officials alike. Each can claim credit for the highways or school lunches or whatevers that the grants help finance and each can point a finger at the other should anything go wrong with them. A program's congressional sponsors can pat themselves on the back for the benefits bestowed on a state and the state officials can point to the fact that it only cost them one dollar of state funds to trigger four dollars' worth of benefits. But if the project turns sour, those officials can place the blame on the rigid federal regulations with which they were forced to comply.

I encountered that complaint with some frequency during my Senate days. New York officials would often note that they were unable to address a particular welfare or other problem as effectively as they would have liked because of the federal rules they were required to apply, and in my experience they were usually right. They were on the scene, knew the relevant facts, and reached common sense judgments on how a particular problem could best be addressed. But they were not allowed to act on their own judgment and therefore could not be held accountable for their failures.

The Supreme Court has recognized the political account-ability problem that attends Congressional mandates in another context. In the landmark 1992 case *New York v. United States*, the Court found that a federal statute requiring the state to take physical possession of radioactive waste was a violation of the Tenth Amendment because it denied New York voters the ability to hold their elected officials responsible for their actions.

> [W]here the Federal Government compels States to regulate, the accountability of both state and federal officials is diminished. If the citizens of New York, for example, do not consider that making provision for the disposal of radioactive waste is in their best interest, they may elect state officials who share their view. That view can always be pre-empted under the Supremacy Clause if it is contrary to the national view, but in such a case it is the Federal Government that makes the decision in full view of the public, and it will be federal officials that suffer the consequences if the decision turns out to be detrimental or unpopular. But where the Federal Government directs the States to regulate, it may be state officials who will bear the brunt of public disapproval, while the federal officials who devised the regulatory program may remain insulated from the electoral ramifications of their decision. Accountability is thus diminished when, due to federal coercion, elected state officials cannot regulate in accordance with the views of the local electorate in matters not pre-empted by federal regulation.

Unfortunately, within the grants-in-aid context, the Supreme Court has been less concerned with the dangers that Justice O'Connor (the author of the *New York* decision and the dissent in *South Dakota v. Dole* that I mentioned earlier) described as "garbled political responsibility."

Another accountability problem arises from what is sometimes referred to as "picket fence federalism," in which different levels of government cooperate in achieving common goals. The horizontal "slats" represent the cooperating federal and state governments while the upright pickets are the projects for which they share responsibility. Where federal grants-in-aid are concerned, the cooperating usually takes place between state and federal agencies, and those manning the former have a tendency to reflect the views of their federal counterparts rather than those of the state officials who are their nominal bosses. The federalized "lawyer's playground" of special education which I discussed above is a good example of this. Although special education teachers and administrators are theoretically local employees, their salaries are largely paid with federal funds and their loyalties tend to follow accordingly. As the 1986 Brookings Institution report "When Federalism Works" has noted, the bond between the federal government and those state employees is so close that Washington has helped finance a special education lobbying organization, the National Association of State Directors of Special Education.

State agencies have also used the leverage of federal funding to achieve changes in state laws, as illustrated in a study by University of Virginia Professor Martha Derthick (*The Influence of Federal Grants*). Massachusetts, like other New England states, had long relied on town selectmen to administer assistance to the poor. In the 1960s, this rankled the state's welfare director, who sought a rule requiring that Massachusetts administrators of the federal Aid to Families with Dependent Children program have college degrees, which was his way of moving welfare administration from the town to the state level. As the Massachusetts legislature, half of whose members then lacked college degrees, was unlikely to oblige him, the director secured a letter from the relevant federal agency instructing him to administer AFDC funding through holders of college degrees. He then worked with federal officials to write legislation for Massachusetts implementing the new requirement. When the legislature balked, the director let it be known that the state would lose federal grant money if it failed to adopt the new rule. Threatened with the loss of federal funds, the state's legislators capitulated.

INEFFICIENCIES ARISING FROM COST EXTERNALIZATION

Anyone who has ever eaten lunch on an expense account will understand the perverse incentives generated when a person is given access to funds that may only be used for a particular purpose. If an employer will reimburse an employee for up to $40 for a lunch, the latter will be tempted to spend all of it on a three-course meal even though he would have paid $15 for a sandwich and cup of coffee if he had been spending his own money. In economic terms, the difference between what he charged to his employer and the $15 he otherwise would have spent for his lunch is known as cost externalization. Economically, this is very inefficient because if the employee had received $40 in cash, he would have spent $15 of it for lunch and used the balance to satisfy other needs with the same attention to cost and acceptable quality that he demonstrated in feeding himself.

Organizations, governments included, will act in the same way. When someone else picks up the check, they consume goods and services inefficiently, which results in higher prices. When their own cash is on the line—that is to say, in the language of economics, when the costs are internalized—they will try to get the best possible price for the goods and services they purchase. Regulation-ridden federal grants have the same effect on their recipients as a lunch allowance has on an employee. In each instance, the recipient uses someone else's money to pay for stipulated purposes.

Rhode Island's recent Medicaid reforms provide a striking illustration of this. Because of the state's horrendous fiscal condition, in January 2009 the federal government granted

Rhode Island a five-year waiver of compliance with Medicaid regulations in exchange for a cap on federal contributions to the program. Before the waiver, the state was subject to federal regulations that controlled the kinds of health care that it could purchase for its Medicaid enrollees. Under the formula in effect at the time, the federal government provided Rhode Island with an open-ended offer to reimburse them for over half of whatever the state spent on the program. Under the circumstances, it is hardly surprising that at the time Rhode Island cut its deal and accepted a cap on grants, the costs of the program rose year after year.

That deal had dramatic consequences. Freed of pettifogging regulations, Rhode Island was able to bring its Medicaid costs under tight control while improving the quality of the medical care it provided enrollees. As the state's former secretary of health and human services, Gary Alexander, has pointed out, the cap on federal funding "changed our culture of spending on Medicaid" because "now wasting money came out of our budget." The 2013 Rhode Island Office of Health and Human Services "Rhode Island Annual Medicaid Expenditure Report" describes the consequences. In the year prior to the waiver, the state's Medicaid cost per enrollee ("PMPM," or per-member-per-month) had grown at a rate of 6.6 percent. In 2009, after the waiver took effect, the state brought the rate of growth down to 1.1 percent. In 2011 and 2012, Rhode Island's Medicaid costs actually declined by 2.3 and 3.1 percent respectively with the result that "[o]verall PMPM costs are lower . . . in 2012 than they were 5 years ago." That is in sharp contrast with the 7.5 percent annual increase in Medicaid costs experienced in the rest of the country over that same period. Rhode Island's success persuaded the Obama administration to extend the waiver for another five years, until December 2018.

While the rest of the country continued to buy the health

care equivalents of $40 lunches on the federal government's tab, Rhode Island's price sensitivity led it to find better-priced health services of an equivalent or better quality. Relaxation of federal regulations allowed its Medicaid services to make greater use of lower-cost home care and assisted living options as alternatives to nursing homes. The state also began to provide Medicaid patients with incentives to seek preventative care and to live healthier lives through the distribution of health club memberships, cash payments, and gift cards that rewarded healthier behavior. An independent study by the Lewin Group, a health care consulting firm, shows that Rhode Island's new policies have lowered emergency room utilization and improved access to physician services for patients with a number of medical problems. The lesson learned from the Rhode Island Medicaid example applies, of course, to every other grants-in-aid program that limits the recipients' options on how to spend federal money.

THREATS TO STATE EXPERIMENTATION

One of the advantages of federalism is that it allows individual states to explore different ways of dealing with responsibilities that they share with the other forty-nine. In the real world there is rarely a "best" way to achieve particular state goals, especially when one takes into consideration the enormous variety in the demographics, topography, and climates of a continental nation with a population of more than 315 million people. If unimpeded by federal regulations, individual states will serve as laboratories in which new approaches to education, or taxation, or welfare, or the construction of highways, can be developed and tested. Successful innovations can then be emulated by the other states and disastrous ones rejected. The problem with the availability of federal grants is that they come with federal rules that impose uniform requirements from sea to shining sea, which impede the ability of the states to test alternatives. If the federal rules prove wrongheaded, they are hard to correct because of the glacial pace of statutory and regulatory reform.

Washington, however, doesn't have to impose its own regulations on the states in order to discourage state-level experimentation. Its co-option of favored state initiatives will have the same effect. The interplay between the federal Race to the Top education program and the states' Common Core initiative is a prime example of this. The National Governors Association and the Council of Chief State School Officers launched Common Core in 2009 with the objective of devising standards that would ensure that American students achieved stipulated levels of proficiency in English and mathematics by the end of each grade from kindergarten through twelfth. In due course, the final Common Core standards were released and the states invited to adopt them.

The federal Race to the Top program also came on the scene in 2009. As described by the Department of Education, the program was a three-phase $4.35 billion "competitive grant program designed to encourage and reward States that are creating the conditions for education innovation and reform." States competing for slices of the $4.35 billion pie were required to describe how they met twenty-eight educational criteria, two of which involved "working toward jointly developing and adopting a common set of K-12 standards." The instructions noted that "'High' points" would be awarded to contestants who, by August 2, 2010, had joined a consortium that included a majority of states. Common Core (the only potential consortium in town) released its standards on June 2, 2010. Forty-one states and the District of Columbia rushed to join the consortium by the Department's deadline and four others soon followed suit.

The National Governors Association complained to the Secretary of Education that the resulting two-month window conflicted "with the timeline agreed to by governors and chief state school officers in the Common Core State Standards Initiative Memorandum of Agreement . . . that states may adopt the common core standards in accordance with state timelines for standards adoption, not to exceed *three years*" (emphasis added). As it was, for a chance to share in the Race to the Top prize money, many states had to abandon their own procedural safeguards. As Senator Charles Grassley noted in a March 2014 letter to his Senate colleagues, "Illinois adopted Common Core by emergency amendment, waiving the required 45 day comment period. Oklahoma adopted the standards by emergency rule, bypassing legislative approval as its legislature was out of session." Mississippi also bypassed the requirements of its own Administrative Procedures Act on a "finding of imminent peril to public welfare in the loss of substantial federal funds from the Race to the Top Grant." It did so in vain. Mississippi was not among the nineteen states that ultimately shared the Race to the Top jackpot.

Defenders of that program note that the federal government had no hand in designing the Common Core standards. That is true. It is also beside the point. Race to the Top pressured the participating states into adopting a set of standards favored though not designed by Washington. In doing so (to quote Senator Grassley's letter), it interfered "with decisions that are properly made at the state and local level, closer to the children affected and their parents." As it happens, now that the program's funds have been disbursed and enough time has elapsed to subject the Common Core standards to critical examination, a number of states are beginning to have second thoughts as to their merits. Virginia withdrew from the competition early on based on the conclusion that its own standards were superior. In early 2014, Indiana also withdrew for the same reason, and several others have since followed suit. Despite these defections, Common Core may well prove a major step forward for American education. If that proves to be the case, the defectors can jump back on board. But the cause of education can only benefit from the fact that some states remain free to pursue their own alternatives. If one of them does develop standards that prove superior to Common Core's, Common Core will be free to adopt them—something that would not be possible if the federal Department of Education had designed the standards and then imposed them on all the states.

Another example of federal co-option is "Aimee's Law" (named for the murdered victim of a sex crime), which was enacted in 2000. The law deals with the sentencing of individuals convicted under state law for the crimes of murder, rape, and "dangerous sexual offenses" as federally defined. It is addressed to cases where someone imprisoned for one of those crimes in one state is subsequently convicted of committing any one of them in another. If the term of imprisonment imposed by the first state was less than the average term imposed by all the states for the same crime, or if the convict had served less than eighty-five percent of the term of imprisonment to which he had been sentenced, the first state will suffer a penalty payable out of a portion of the federal law enforcement funds it would otherwise receive.

Punishing a state for awarding shorter sentences than the average imposed nationally for the same offense provides a perverse incentive for states to keep increasing the severity of the punishments awarded for those crimes. Lenient states are placed under pressure to increase their mandatory sentences. In doing so, however, they raise the bar by lengthening the national average prison term for those offenses, which, in turn, causes other states to increase theirs. As Senator Russ Feingold put it during the Senate debate of the measure, "[h]ere, of course, we are not preparing to pass a new federal murder, rape, or sexual offense statute. But we might as well do that because in Aimee's Law we are forcing the states through the use of federal law enforcement assistance funds to increase their penalties for these offenses. . . . Basically, this policy could force states to either enact the death penalty or never release a person convicted of murder on parole."

Where they are free to examine alternatives without the risk of incurring penalties, however, the states have been moving in the opposite direction. They have learned that the "throw away the key" approach to criminal justice can be counterproductive. There is substantial evidence, for example, that beyond a certain point, imprisonment will increase the risk of recidivism. In the case of lesser crimes than those that are the subject of Aimee's Law, such as drug possession, there may be alternatives to incarceration, such as treatment, that both serve the needs of justice and are far more likely to return convicted individuals to a useful place in society. A 2011 ACLU report, "Smart Reform Is Possible," described criminal justice reforms across the country—from California to Texas to Ohio—that are reducing the states' bloated prison populations by doing away with mandatory minimum sentencing and reducing prison penalties for nonviolent offenders. What is clear is that imprisonment for imprisonment's sake can be very costly in both dollars and human terms. Federal incentives like Aimee's Law, however, discourage states from reconsidering what the appropriate penalties are for the crimes to which they apply.

State experimentation remains the best way to develop more effective ways of delivering public services. The surest way to kill state initiatives, however, is to impose federal regulatory straitjackets on them. That is the inescapable consequence of grants-in-aid programs that now extend over virtually every area of state responsibility.

COSTS INHERENT IN A SECOND LEVEL
OF GOVERNMENT

Federal grants programs add a second layer of government to the design and administration of activities conducted at the state level; and when a grant is routed through a state to a subsidiary government, as is often the case, there will be a third. In assessing the cost of the federal layer, one must take into account the fact that government is by nature monopolistic, rigid, and political. That is largely true of state as well as federal governments, although unlike the latter, the states are in competition with one another. As this book is focused on the effects of federal grants, my discussion here will focus on the government that created them.

Because the federal government is a monopoly, it is not subject to the disciplines of the marketplace that, in the private sector, promote efficiency and weed out losers. If costs exceed budget, Washington will raise taxes or borrow money to pay for the overruns; and if a program fails to achieve its goals, too often the congressional response is to throw more money at it. The programs are rigid because Congress will rarely admit that one was ill-advised and cancel it: on the contrary, even the worst programs are protected by an "iron triangle" consisting of the legislators who created it, the bureaucrats who administer it, and the groups who benefit from the status quo, however flawed. While private enterprises and individuals are able to respond overnight to new circumstances and act quickly to correct errors in judgment, once a regulatory regimen is locked in place, it is enormously difficult to modify. All federal programs are subject to congressional oversight, of course, but Congress is too preoccupied with current agendas to scrutinize the management of more than a fraction of the programs it has created.

Then there is the matter of politics. Because Congress is a political animal, it is inevitable that where there is a conflict between politics and common sense or Economics 101, politics will usually decide the issue. Career legislators are extremely reluctant to take any action that would offend important constituencies. To cite some typical examples, it is conceded (and the experience of states like Texas confirms) that tort reform would reduce medical costs by tens of billions of dollars, but lest tort lawyers be offended, that most obvious reform was ignored by congressional committees intent on a trillion-dollar restructuring of health care; a handful of sugar-beet farmers are kept in business by restrictions on the importation of cane sugar that cost 315 million American consumers around $2 billion a year more than they would have to pay if they could buy their sugar at prevailing world prices; and to protect manufacturers in their constituencies, Republican and Democratic congressmen exhibit rare bipartisanship in continuing the production of weapons that the Pentagon no longer wants.

Nor can it be assumed that individuals enlisted in federal service are more dedicated to the disinterested pursuit of the public good than those working for states. Whatever their pedigrees, human beings are—human. That is true of the elected representatives who enact our laws, the experts on whom they rely in crafting them, and the administrators who man the agencies and bureaus that issue the regulations required to implement them. While it is assumed that all of those individuals will pursue an objective public good as they carry out their responsibilities, the insights of "public choice" analyses have tossed buckets of cold water on those happy assumptions. They confirm that consciously or unconsciously, those legislators, experts, and administrators tend to weigh the costs and benefits of any action in ways that advance their own well-being as measured by such rewards as safeguarding careers, the achievement of ideological goals, or the acquisition of power. They pursue the public good as they understand it, but that understanding will tend to coincide with their own self-interest.

Academia spins out yards of disinterested studies proposing ways of resolving a vast variety of public concerns. When academics find their way into positions in Washington where they can put their proposals into effect, however, their best intentions are subject to subversion. In "The Politicization of Society," Ronald M. Hartwell suggests that

> Intellectuals dislike [classical] liberalism because the market economy does not reward them according to their own estimate of their obvious social worth. Intellectuals, therefore, prefer economic systems which give them a place in the sun, in which their cash rewards are almost certainly higher, and in which power rewards are undoubtedly higher. Intellectuals play leading roles in the bureaucracies of the state, as advisors, experts, and administrators, and increasing the power of the state means increasing the power of the intellectuals.

That is one explanation—an overly harsh one, I suspect—of why the panaceas spun out of academe so often require the creation of government programs with all their attendant regulations.

Those who administer our regulatory agencies are subject to influences of a special kind. Their careers are focused on advancing their agencies' goals and this will inevitably affect their perspectives. Consider the concerns over the public's right of privacy that were raised by the 2013 disclosure that the National Security Agency had acquired the ability to intercept virtually all domestic telephone calls. The NSA's mission is the critical one of detecting potential terrorist threats against the United States, so it should not be surprising if its personnel place a greater importance on that mission than on the possibility that an intelligence official might infringe on privacy by listening in on your conversations or mine.

The same mission bias can be expected of other agencies. The EPA's concern for the protection of the environment tends to blind it to the ways a proposed regulation could adversely affect other equally legitimate interests. Federal agencies and bureaus are charged with balancing costs against benefits when they issue new rules, but those costs and benefits are often difficult to quantify. So it should surprise no one if regulators place a greater value on the interests they are in the business of advancing than they do on competing ones. None of this argues against the need for government safeguards in appropriate areas. It merely suggests that central planners are no more exempt from human frailties than anyone else.

The impact of self-interest on public service is nowhere more evident than in Congress, whose members must seek reelection every two or six years. Thus from their first days in office, senators and members of the House of Representatives are conscious of the imperative need to create records that will ensure their reelection. That political reality was brought home to me when, shortly after I took my oath of office as a United States senator, I attended a meeting for newly elected Republicans that had been called by Senator John Tower in his capacity as chairman of the Senate Republican Campaign Committee. After congratulating us on our election, he said, "Gentlemen, it is important for you to understand that your first responsibility is to ensure your reelection."

This focus on reelection and the deviations from principle that such a focus encourages are now part of the congressional culture. Today's members are full-time career legislators, and the protection of a career is an understandable human imperative. That was not always the case. During the first two-thirds of our national existence, members of Congress were citizen-legislators who would usually spend less than six months in Washington and then return to their homes and resume their normal lives as lawyers or farmers or businessmen during the balance of the year. Today, however, Congress is in session virtually the entire year, and its members are heavily engaged in constituent work during their much-criticized spring and summer breaks. Ensuring that their careers are not cut short inevitably influences everything they do, and much of what they now do is at the expense of their core responsibilities under the Constitution.

In his book *The Debt Bomb*, Senator Coburn provides a biting analysis of the ways that "careerism" consumes congressional energies. A prime task of any congressional office is to churn out press releases that will be published in local papers, and members have found the most effective way of doing this is to find ways of channeling federal money into their districts or states. This has resulted in a "parochialism" (to borrow Senator Coburn's word) that, on his arrival in the Senate in 2005, was evidenced by the practice of attaching "earmarks" to appropriations bills requiring that funds committed to existing grants-in-aid programs be spent on projects of optimum constituent appeal. This practice became so popular that their number rose from 3,023 in 1996 to 15,877 in 2006, a fivefold increase in just ten years.

Those allocations had little to do with national priorities, but the practice of attaching earmarks had come to be viewed as a legislator's right. This was made nakedly apparent in the controversy that arose over the notorious "Bridge to Nowhere," an earmark created by Alaska Senator Ted Stevens that directed the expenditure of $223 million on the construction of a bridge linking Ketchikan, Alaska with sparsely populated Gravina Island, home of Ketchikan International Airport, despite the fact that the island was adequately served by ferry. Newcomer Senator Coburn questioned the merits of that expenditure and had the temerity to introduce an amendment that would apply those $223 million to the urgent work of cleaning up after Hurricane Katrina. This led to an extraordinarily revealing response from Senator Stevens:

> I have been here now almost 37 years. This is the first time I have seen any attempt by any Senator to treat my State in a way differently from any other State. It will not happen. . . . I have never seen it suggested to single out one State and say, you pay for a disaster that happened 5,000 miles away. . . . [W]hat is being done to our State has never been done to any other State.

In other words, in Senator Stevens' view and in that of the large majority of other senators who joined him in opposing the Coburn amendment, earmarks had the status of proprietary rights to which each member of Congress was entitled, and no one should dare tamper with them. So it is hardly surprising that the amendment was defeated by a vote of 82 to 15. Congress might consider the more forthright approach of the Philippine Congress, which, until recently, provided its members with specified amounts of public money each year for deployment as they saw fit.

The Bridge to Nowhere and other such abuses, however, had so stigmatized earmarks that, in 2010, Congress agreed to suspend the practice during the balance of the 112th Congress. As Senator Coburn noted in his book, that did not prevent congressional offices from applying pressures on agencies to ensure that their constituencies secured larger slices of the grants-in-aid pies. And I don't see how they can be criticized for doing so. A federal program for the repair of dilapidated bridges, for example, will never be endowed with sufficient funds to restore every bridge in the United States. It is therefore entirely understandable that members of Congress will feel an obligation to ensure that their states secure a fair share of the appropriated funds.

The merit of eliminating the federal layer of government

in state and local affairs goes beyond the baggage that I have described. Putting a federal agency in charge of a program capable of being handled by the states imposes a cost of its own. This was strikingly illustrated in a 2012 *Wall Street Journal* editorial by Senator (and former Tennessee governor) Lamar Alexander proposing a Grand Swap in which the federal government assumed total responsibility for Medicaid while the states did the same for K-12 education. He stated that this would enhance the quality of education because

> State and local leaders know best how to create an environment in which students can learn what they need to know to succeed in college and in careers.... While Washington has provided some important advocacy and requirements for better reporting of test scores, most of the initiative for higher standards, better tests, more accountability and more parental choice has come from the states.

While some will challenge those assertions, they cannot be dismissed out of hand, given the senator's credentials as a former U.S. Secretary of Education and president of the University of Tennessee.

Senator Alexander also noted that the Grand Swap had the potential for strengthening Medicaid: A single manager, even if it is the federal government, would operate Medicaid more efficiently because it would be forced to implement the mandates it crafts. That is a wise observation applicable to every existing grants program, but it doesn't mean that a single federal manager would be any more efficient than a single manager at the state level, as my earlier description of Rhode Island's Medicaid experience has demonstrated.

There is one central lesson to be drawn from Senator Alexander's insights and Rhode Island's successful management of its Medicaid program, and that is that placing total responsibility for the design and funding of a government program in one set of hands is the best guarantee that it will be conducted wisely, and that where there is an option, the states will usually assure us the optimum results. The reason for this is simple: circumstances vary so greatly from state to state in a country as vast as ours that it is highly improbable that a single set of rules can serve the best interests of all fifty of them, and the officials who are the closest to a problem are in the best position to resolve it. As with all rules, this one has its potential exceptions. There is no reason, for example, why Washington should not assume sole responsibility for the maintenance and expansion of the Interstate Highway System. By definition, it serves a national purpose beyond the competence of individual states and it falls within the federal government's powers under Interstate Commerce Clause. What is important is that only one level of government be involved. That not only eliminates many of the costs I have described but leaves no question as to who is responsible for the manner in which the responsibilities are met.

THE COST TO CONGRESS

Once upon a time, the United States Senate was known as both the world's greatest deliberative body and its most exclusive club. The first suggests that senators went about their legislative duties with great care, that they attended the floor debates of pending legislation, studied the proposed laws' merits, and cast their votes based on an informed understanding of their purposes and likely effects. The second description suggests that senators had sufficient leisure to develop friendships across party lines, which made it easier for them to bridge partisan differences. However accurate those characterizations may have been in years long past, they bear little relationship to today's Senate, and they cannot because of the extraordinary pressures under which its members are now forced to live.

Shortly after my election to the Senate in 1970, I was handed a recently completed study of Congress that had concluded that the workload of the average congressional office had doubled every five years since 1935. Given the fact that, in simpler times, Congress worked at a leisurely pace and was in session for five or six months a year, its members could take the initial increases in stride simply by devoting more hours per day and more months per year to their work. Over time, however, the available hours and months were exhausted, and the doubling could only be accommodated by squeezing deliberation out of the legislative process. I can certify that during my own six years in office, I witnessed both a sharp increase in the already frenetic pace of the Senate and an equally sharp decline in its ability to get very much done that could honestly be labeled "thoughtful."

This pressure cooker existence is the result of Congress's assumption of ever-wider responsibilities, as evidenced by the explosion of federal laws and regulations that began with the New Deal. In 1934, the United States Code consisted of a single volume containing 2,275 pages of statutes, the work product of our Congress's first 137 years. In 1970, when I was elected to the Senate, the Code had grown to eleven volumes, and the 2006 edition contains thirty. But those statutes are just the tip of the iceberg, because they are supplemented by an ever-expanding number of small print regulations that have the force of law and currently fill 235 volumes that occupy more than 24 feet of shelf space. Those laws and regulations touch virtually every corner of American life, with the result that individuals and communities increasingly encounter problems that require them to deal with Washington, and so they turn to their congressional representatives for help.

This combination of legislative and constituent work has converted Congress from an institution that could once think problems through to responsible conclusions into a treadmill that is turning at an accelerating pace. That treadmill is now spinning out of control. I recall a *Washington Post* article a few years ago by a reporter who had acted as a congressman's shadow over the course of a week. He reported that the poor man had no more than fifteen minutes a day for consecutive thought. If that seems implausible, consider a typical congressman's daily schedule as reported by the nonpartisan Congressional Management Foundation and the Society for Human Resource Management in their 2013 report "Life in Congress: The Member Perspective," based on their survey of twenty-five members of the House (see page 50).

This sample schedule is instructive in several ways. It illustrates the frenetic pace of congressional service as well as the fact that most meetings are too brief to permit members to discuss their subject matter in any depth. Staff members brief representatives on the meetings' purposes as they run from one engagement to the next. The staffers will then stay on and later prepare memoranda regarding the substance of the meetings that their principals may or may not find time to read. About half the substantive meetings (examples would be the meetings with the National Women, Infants, and Children Association representatives, on fingerprinting for food stamps, and with the local county representatives and supervisors) involve matters in which federal grants could come into play. It is worth noting that time is also set aside for raising money for the next reelection campaign, which has become a daily congressional preoccupation.

"Life in Congress: The Member Perspective" also noted that members work seventy-hour weeks when Congress is in session and slow down to fifty-nine-hour weeks during recesses. It observed that members juggle several committee hearings and various meetings occurring simultaneously during the day. Based on my own experience, that means that members will either ignore one committee meeting completely or make

SAMPLE HOUSE MEMBER SCHEDULE
MARCH 6, 2012

Following is a sample schedule of one day in a house member's Washington, D.C., office. *Only identifying details have been altered.*

9:00 AM–9:30 AM	National Women, Infants, and Children's Association *Speak to attendees of 2012 Leadership Conference.*
10:00 AM–12:00 PM	Agriculture, Rural Development, Food and Drug Administration, and Related Agencies Appropriations Hearing *Marketing Regulatory Programs.*
10:30 AM–12:00 PM	Bipartisan classified national security briefing *Briefing on Iran.*
12:00 PM–1:00 PM	Caucus/conference meeting with Democratic/Republican colleagues *Jobs, the economy and gas prices.*
12:45 PM–1:15 PM	Edie Smith, local county WIC (Women, Infant, Children) program manager *Update on WIC issues and funding for FY13.*
1:15 PM–1:45 PM	Representatives from the American Israel Public Affairs Committee (AIPAC) *Discuss the U.S.-Israel relationship including aid to Israel, Iran's nuclear quest, and the Israeli-Palestinian peace process.*
1:30 PM–2:00 PM	Kevin Jones, local county supervisor *Discuss H.R. 3460, the National Parks Lands Bill.*
2:00 PM–2:30 PM	Bob Ellis, Solutions for Progress nonprofit *Discuss fingerprinting for Supplemental Nutrition Assistance Program in our state.*
2:30 PM–3:00 PM	U.S. Army/local officials *Discuss land transfer issues.*
3:00 PM–4:00 PM	Fundraising call time—Party HQ
3:00 PM–3:30 PM	FYI: Army Corps of Engineers, Regional District *Discuss current projects.*
3:30 PM–4:00 PM	Organic Farming Research Foundation *Discuss farming and conservation programs.*
4:30 PM–5:00 PM	Vanessa Garcia, local supervisor *Discuss health issues as well as local county's legislative priorities*
5:00 PM–6:00 PM	Local county representatives/supervisors *Discuss flood control efforts, the local gang intervention program, and the National Monument designation.*
6:30 PM–9:30 PM	FYI: American Council for Capital Formation dinner discussion *"The 2012 Election: Impact on the U.S. Deficit & Economy, Tax, Regulatory and Energy Policy."*

token appearances at each. Either way, they are unable to participate fully in the committee work that is their primary institutional responsibility. But that is the nature of the job today, a job that the report likens to "the hectic world of an emergency room physician." That is a perceptive analogy. But if you have serious health problems, will you take them to the emergency room or to a doctor who has had the time to study and reflect and to consider the consequences of alternative courses of treatment?

One result of this treadmill existence is Congress's increasing habit of ducking the exacting details that might require members of the House and Senate to think legislative initiatives through to their practical consequences. Instead, they assign essentially legislative responsibilities to the unelected men and women who staff the agencies that issue the regulations that determine how the new law will affect our lives. Prime examples of this reckless approach to lawmaking are the 906-page Affordable Care and 849-page Dodd-Frank Wall Street and Consumer Protection Acts that were signed into law in 2010. Four years have since elapsed, and as of this writing a large number of the regulations mandated by those acts have yet to be released. In the case of Dodd-Frank, by September 2014, only 220 of the required 398 rulemakings had been finalized and another 95 had yet to be proposed. Only when all the regulations are in place will the public, let alone the members of Congress who voted the acts into law, have a clear idea of what they will cost and how they will affect the delivery of health and financial services. This is hardly the way a responsible legislative body should go about its business.

Congress has shown itself equally irresponsible in what it has failed to address. To cite one glaring example, for over a dozen years Democrats and Republicans alike have known that the escalating costs of our Social Security, Medicare, and Medicaid programs must be brought under control if we are to escape a financial meltdown. It is a simple question of math. In 2012, the federal government distributed $1.23 trillion to Social Security and Medicare beneficiaries. But current wage earners, through their payroll texes, only paid $845 billion into the system. That left a nearly $400 billion deficit that is being financed through the sale of Treasury bonds our grandchildren will have to redeem (Budget of the U.S. Government, Fiscal Year 2014, Historical Tables). The reasons for this are simple. In 1935, when Social Security was launched, the life expectancy of Americans was 61.7 years; by 2010, it had increased to 78.7 years. In 1960, 5.1 workers were paying payroll taxes into the fund for every retired individual. Today there are 2.9. Yet nothing is done to adjust the law to demographic reality because tinkering with Social Security remains the third rail of American politics. Instead, thanks to the Supreme Court's Spending Clause decisions, Congress can focus on such politically benign matters as helping the states shelter their homeless and feed their poor.

It is hard to determine what percentage of a member's time is currently consumed directly or indirectly with grants to states, but a study published by the Hoover Institution in 1963 reported that "[a] review of the *Congressional Record* shows that most of the time of Congress is spent on approving numerous types of local benefits" (W. Glenn Campbell, "Assuring the Primacy of National Security"). If that was true in 1963 when fewer than three hundred federal grants programs were in effect, one must assume that a significant proportion of congressional time is still being devoted to drafting new ones, funding existing ones, and ensuring that constituents receive appropriate shares of the funds at the programs' disposal.

According to the survey of a representative group of congressmen in "Life in Congress," ninety-five percent of them consider staying in touch with constituents to be their most important responsibility, and they devote twenty-four percent of their nonadministrative work time on "constituent services work" while in Washington and fifty-two percent when they are home in their districts. All of that is laudable. But I think it a fair guess that the average constituent is more concerned about his housing, highways, and the education of his children (all the subjects of federal grants) than he is about such issues as the defense budget, environmental regulation, and our Mideast policy. So long as the Supreme Court sanctions congressional action in areas that are the responsibilities of governors and mayors, members of Congress will understandably cater to such concerns.

THE COST TO THE PEOPLE

I live in Sharon, Connecticut, a town of 3,000. A three-man Board of Selectmen and a handful of subsidiary boards that deal with such matters as our school, zoning, housing, and finances govern the town. Issues of any importance are discussed in open town hall meetings and are decided by majority vote of those attending. If the meeting's subject is, for example, the desirability of paving a dirt road, those in attendance will know the relevant facts and make informed judgments as to whether the money could be put to better use. This is government of, by, and for the people in its purest form. If a problem involves a state law or proposal, we do not have the same access to those in authority, but if we join with others who share our concerns, we have a reasonable chance of securing a hearing at the state capitol. Furthermore, we can easily catch the ear of our state senator and representative. They are very accessible, and because they are familiar with our part of the state, they understand what we are talking about, and we can hold them responsible for their performance on election day.

The problem today is that those governing our towns and

states are no longer in control of a large proportion of the government activities that affect our lives. In too many respects, our state officials now serve as administrators of programs designed in Washington by civil servants who are beyond our reach, immune to the discipline of the ballot box, and the least informed about our particular conditions and needs. And that explains the frustrations felt by the inhabitants of the two communities served by the one-lane bridge I mentioned earlier.

The bridge was closed in April 2012. Those who most often used it have made it clear that they want it replaced by another one-lane structure for reasons of public safety peculiar to its location and its use by pedestrians and bicyclists. In order to avail themselves of eighty percent federal financing, however, their selectmen had to present their case to the Connecticut highway authorities in Hartford who, in turn, submitted it to the federal agency in charge of such grants. Time passeth and costs and frustrations mount. Eventually, after discussing the possibility of a waiver with Washington, Hartford advised the towns that as the replacement would last more than seventy years, state policy required that it have two or more lanes. Connecticut's policy may well be the wise one, but because federal funding was involved, the state first had to consult with federal functionaries over the merits of one versus two lanes before it announced its own position.

So it is back to the drawing board. A new design for the bridge will in time be presented to Hartford and, if Hartford approves, it will be passed on to Washington for final scrutiny. If Connecticut had been the source of financing, the people of the two communities and the state highway authorities would have reached a decision on how to proceed long ago and work on the necessary restoration could now be underway. And the irony is that the eighty percent federal financing, when it eventually materializes, will represent nothing more than a return of money that was sent to Washington by Connecticut taxpayers, less a substantial surcharge for the round trip.

This is just one example of a grant application in progress, and it involves a very modest one at that The process, however, is the same whether the amount sought is one million or one billion dollars. And as my example demonstrates, it relegates the members of the affected communities to the role of helpless bystanders. While the town selectmen in my example were able to discuss the pros and cons of a one-lane bridge with state officials, those at the federal level were beyond their reach. The people who decide how the money will be used lie beyond the reach of the people the grants are intended to benefit, and the purported beneficiaries have no say in the matter. The loss of that control is a most serious cost to Americans who still believe in self-government.

IN SUM

What an examination of a fifty-year record has established is that the most costly and least efficient way to build a county road or provide medical care for the poor is to entrust fundamental decision-making tasks to officials who are the farthest removed from the work site or clinic. Yet the creation and nurture of grants-in-aid programs has become a brutally expensive addiction. A congressman touring his district will hear a woman complain about her city's shoddy garbage collection. On his return to Washington, his reflexive response will be to introduce legislation authorizing subsidies for communities purchasing garbage trucks that meet federal specifications. His constituent will swoon over the prompt reaction to her complaint and her local paper will praise the congressman's attention to his constituents' problems. It is a win-win game—except for the taxpayers who have to foot the bill and the mayor who would rather have spent his city's funds on more pressing needs.

Those programs' costs in dollars, costs in misdirected priorities, costs in overlapping administration, costs in rigid one-size-fits-all regulation, and the citizens' loss of control over government actions that most directly affect them should satisfy any objective observer that they represent the most misguided means of providing public services that lie within the states' acknowledged areas of competence. It is time that Congress kicked the habit.

★ 4 ★

A MODEST PROPOSAL

In 1729, Jonathan Swift published a blistering satire entitled *A Modest Proposal for Preventing the Children of Poor People From Being a Burthen to Their Parents or Country, and For Making Them Beneficial to The Publick.* His proposal was simplicity itself: eat the children. His sober discussion of their preparation for market and probable price per pound was intended to do no more than shock his readers into an awareness of the condition of the Irish and of British policies that kept them in poverty. He would have been appalled if anyone had taken his proposal at face value.

Unlike Swift, I expect my proposal to be taken very seriously. Nevertheless, despite its demonstrable reasonableness, the political establishment will find it as outrageous as Swift's because my call for the abolition of all federal grants-in-aid programs threatens so many of their interests. It will deny members of Congress their easiest paths to reelection, threaten the jobs of the thousands of employees of the federal agencies and bureaus that oversee the programs, deprive governors and mayors of their readiest access to funds they don't have to raise from their own taxpayers, and distress the hordes of special interests that rely on the programs to impose their goals on state and local governments.

My proposal warrants serious consideration because no other single reform offers so sure a way of achieving so many public goods. If adopted, it will reduce federal spending by more than one-sixth and eliminate a major diversion of congressional time and energy from such trivia as balancing the federal budget, reforming entitlement and tax laws, and bringing runaway bureaucracies under some degree of control. It will also liberate state officials from federal regulations that increase the cost and decrease the effectiveness of their work, and enable our citizens to regain control over governmental actions that most directly affect them.

THE PROPOSAL

Specifically, what I propose is that Congress immediately terminate all federal programs that offer grants to states and their subdivisions. I emphasize the "all" because if any exception is made, members of Congress will be encouraged to launch a new generation of grants on the assurance that theirs will be exempt from all the problems and costs that I have cataloged, and it would take another generation to prove them wrong.

Because federal grants currently constitute more than thirty percent of state revenues, Congress cannot cut off the flow of federal money overnight. Therefore, I propose that it terminate the grants by converting them into single no-strings-attached block grants, one for each state, that would be phased out over a period of five or six years. That would allow ample time for Congress and the states to adjust their respective tax codes to accommodate the successive reductions in the federal transfers. Increases in taxes paid to the states would be offset by reductions in the money taxpayers send to Washington. This may sound like a formidable task, but it shouldn't be. Washington and the states derive their tax revenues from the same sources—the individuals and businesses located in the fifty states and the District of Columbia. It will merely require adjustments in the destinations of their tax payments.

If Congress adopts this proposal, it will phase out over $700 billion of current federal expenditures (the $640.8 billion in federal grants estimated for FY 2015 plus an estimate of more than $60 billion in federal administration costs) and take a major step towards balancing the nation's books. It will also eliminate the substantial costs associated with the overlapping federal and state administration of those programs, take a giant step towards restoring the allocation of governmental duties envisioned by the Constitution's framers, and return full control over state and local governments to their citizens. Most significantly, if it adopts this one reform, Congress will rid itself of a major distraction from its national responsibilities.

The one substantive argument against my proposal is that it would eliminate a ready means for redistributing money from wealthier states to the poorer ones, not that existing programs can be counted upon to spread that money equitably. As the Advisory Commission on Intergovernmental Relations has observed in *An Agenda for American Federalism*, "the record indicates that federal aid programs have never consistently transferred income to the poorest jurisdictions." Nevertheless, the argument in favor of the grants programs as instruments of redistribution must be met As the statistics in Appendix B indicate, the average per capita income of the ten poorest states is 67.6 percent of that of the ten richest. On the face of it, that is a strong argument for asking the latter to help the former meet the cost of providing their residents with acceptable levels of services. The average cost of living in the ten poorest states, however, is 78.6 percent of that of the ten richest ones, which significantly narrows the gap between them, especially when one considers the anomalies that exist in individual cases. To cite an extreme example, Mississippi's per capita income is 75 percent of Hawaii's, but its cost of living is only 55 percent of the latter's. I doubt, though, that anyone will suggest that Mississippians, who inhabit our poorest state, should send care packages to Hawaii, which is our 17th richest.

Redistribution, then, is a weak argument in favor of the existing programs, especially when one takes into account the regulatory freight they carry with them. But if redistribution is indeed a proper function of the federal government, there is a far better way to achieve that goal without imposing webs of federal regulations on all the states, rich and poor alike. My brother William F. Buckley, Jr. proposed a simple means of redistribution in his 1973 book, *Four Reforms*. In his discussion of federal welfare programs, he noted the inherent idiocy of returning money to the wealthier states with instructions on how they can best meet their own welfare needs. He therefore proposed that all federal social welfare grants programs be scrapped and, in their stead, that the federal government provide the have-not states with block grants having the sole requirement that the recipients use the money for welfare. Under that approach, Washington would not be telling the states how to meet their own responsibilities. Nor could it use the needs of the poorer states to impose federal regulations on the wealthier ones.

THE PROPOSAL'S PROSPECTS

The political landscape is riddled with the corpses of proposals for saving the Republic, some of them with the most elegant sponsorships. They are typically contained in reports issued by presidential commissions directed to address problems that Congress has been unwilling or unable to resolve. After months of diligent work by impressively credentialed individuals, the commissions issue their recommendations. Those are discussed by political commentators, usually favorably, and ignored by both the presidents who appointed the commissions and the Congresses that have the power to put them into effect.

That was the fate of the bipartisan commission appointed by President Obama in 2010 to resolve the budgetary deadlock that had paralyzed Washington since the first days of his administration. President Bill Clinton's former Chief of Staff, Erskine Bowles, and former Republican Senator Alan Simpson headed the commission. In due course, and after a great deal of labor, the Bowles-Simpson Commission produced a thoughtful report that included recommendations for bringing a degree of control over the entitlement programs that threaten to bankrupt us and adjusting the federal tax codes to reduce tax rates while increasing revenues through the elimination or revision of a variety of deductions.

When the commission unveiled its proposals, Senator Simpson observed that its plan was "the only one that irritates everybody"; therefore, it was "the only one that will work." Although equal numbers of Democratic and Republican commission members voted for the plan, its proposals for imposing a degree of fiscal discipline on Social Security and Medicare appalled too many Democrats, and too many Republicans rejected any thought of raising tax revenues even though the investment-inhibiting top marginal rates would have been reduced. As a consequence, although its recommendations had great merit, the commission's report was ignored by the president and Congress alike. It had irritated too many people.

In light of the above, how do I have the audacity to believe that my proposal has any better chance of being accepted? On the face of it, it will irritate an even broader range of interests than the political partisans to whom Senator Simpson was referring. But unlike the Bowles-Simpson recommendations, my proposal will not irritate everybody. It will merely appall the political establishment and the private interests that benefit from grants-in-aid programs. On the other hand, once they understand my proposal's implications, Americans across the political spectrum will be able to embrace my reform both as taxpayers and citizens: as taxpayers because of its demonstrable savings at both the federal and state levels, and as citizens because it will return so many decisions on public policy and expenditures to levels of government over which they have the greatest control.

I can say this because Americans reviewing the impact of our grants-in-aid programs over the past fifty years can be expected to reach the following common sense conclusions:

- Washington's experts have proven no better able to help the homeless, or educate a child, or resolve any other state or local problem than the officials who have been elected to take charge of those responsibilities.

- The programs waste tens of billions of dollars a year that the states can put to more effective uses—or leave in their taxpayers' pockets.

- In a country as large as ours, one size can't fit all.

- The money states receive from Washington isn't free. It comes from the federal taxes we pay or from borrowed funds that our children will have to repay.

- Easy money is the enemy of prudent spending.

- Ordinary citizens can't influence federal bureaucracies, but they can still get a hearing at city hall.

- Members of Congress should stop wasting their time on matters that can be handled better at the state and local levels; they should focus on matters that are their exclusive responsibility.

Those points are easily grasped, and an aroused electorate is capable of political miracles. Given the growing disgust with the status quo in Washington, the distrust of federal panaceas that has been triggered by Obamacare's cascading costs, and the simplicity of my proposed reform, I believe it can provide the focal point for a nationwide grassroots demand for meaningful reform.

Furthermore, something in the intellectual air suggests that my timing may be right. In July 2014, for example, *The Atlantic* published an article by Richard A. Epstein and Mario Loyola titled "The United State of America," addressing the federal government's assumption of state responsibilities. The article describes in devastating detail the "intrusive conditions and coercive penalties" inherent in federal assistance programs. The August 2014 issue of *The American*, the online magazine of the American Enterprise Institute, contained an article by Arnold Kling describing the parallel approaches to welfare reform proposed by Republican Congressman Paul Ryan and the left-of-center Brookings Institution's Hamilton Project, which recently issued an e-book, *Policies to Address Poverty in America*. Mr. Kling notes "a close alignment of Ryan's block-grant approach with the many instances in which the authors of the Hamilton Project volume propose flexible, low-cost, small-scale locally administered programs, rather than large-scale, federally administered universal solutions."

For all of these reasons, and because my proposal is based not on ideology but on an objective evaluation of fifty years of experience with federal grants to the states, I believe there is a good chance that it will receive a decent hearing. All that is required is that its merits be fairly debated. It is my hope that this book will trigger that debate.

★ 5 ★

ANCILLARY MEASURES

The problems my proposal is designed to correct have their origins in that old devil, human nature—the combination of hubris, self-interest, and thirst for power that the authors of our Constitution had gone to such pains to contain. Thanks to the Supreme Court's expansive constructions of the Constitution's Commerce and Spending Clauses, we have lost the critical safeguard provided by the Tenth Amendment's clearly stated limits on federal authority. My proposed reform will restore some of those limits, but only for as long as Congress remains chastised and is not distracted by the need to protect careers.

To that end, I now offer two auxiliary reforms as well as an approach to federalism that is both consistent with most of the Supreme Court's precedents and suitable for our times. Because the old temptations will remain as long as members can view congressional service as a lifetime career, the first reform would limit the years they would be permitted to remain in office. And because an amendment of the existing law governing campaign financing can assure them of the money they need for reelection campaigns, my second would relieve them of the need to beg for it personally on a daily basis by lifting caps on individual contributions to candidates. Even with these in place, we need a reaffirmation of federalism reasonably consistent with Supreme Court precedent that will better control the eternal urge to expand federal authority at the expense of the states. To that end, I have the temerity to suggest that the Court may wish to review a critical Spending Clause precedent.

I recognize that it is easier to suggest reforms than put them in place. Mine face formidable problems. Term limits will require a constitutional amendment; lifting the caps on individual campaign donations means congressional incumbents will face better-financed challengers; and the Supreme Court rarely retreats from long-established precedent. Those are substantial obstacles to important reforms, but they warrant the attempt.

TERM LIMITS

Some years ago, I was invited to speak at a Senate prayer breakfast. In my remarks, I noted that, thanks to life tenure, federal judges (which I then was) were immune to one overwhelming temptation that faces elected officials: the temptation to conclude that it is more important for their constituents that they be reelected than that they deal honestly with them; witness the frequency with which legislators yield to political pressures or expediency and vote against their convictions. I then suggested that "given the difficulty of resisting such temptations over the longer run, a proper concern for the welfare of congressional souls may well be the ultimate argument in favor of term limitations."

I doubt that I saved any souls that morning, and not because those attending that prayer breakfast were other than honorable public servants. The problem lies with the fact that Congress has developed its own understanding of acceptable behavior. If one believes he is right on the critical issues of public policy, cutting corners to improve the chances of reelection is surely in the public's interest. This prevailing assumption was brought home to me in late 1975. The bell had rung calling us to the Senate floor to vote on a finance bill that I had never heard of. As was my practice on such occasions, I sought out a member of the Finance Committee whose judgment I trusted. When I asked him to explain the legislation, he replied, "This bill is no good, Jim; but you're from New York and are coming up for election next year, so you should vote 'Aye.'" I was unable to follow his prudent advice, and so found myself casting a rather lonely vote.

I can't claim consistent purity, however. I remember an occasion when a politically appealing motherhood bill had come up for a vote that, on complicated analysis, was very bad policy. Faced with the inability to explain its flaws to constituents in less than a dozen pages of finely honed logic, I voted "Aye." A few minutes later, a political soul mate whose seat was in the row ahead of mine also voted for the bill. After doing so, he turned to me and said, "I feel unclean." And so did I. Such are the pressures of elective office, pressures that can be brought under some control by placing limits on the length of elective service so that in their final terms, at least, members of Congress will feel free to vote their convictions.

My epiphany on that subject had occurred in November 1970. President Nixon had invited me to meet with him shortly after my election to the Senate. When I was ushered into the Oval Office, Nixon was completing a meeting with George Shultz, then director of the Office of Management and Budget, and John Erlichman, who was the president's domestic affairs advisor. As I entered, I heard Nixon say, "But Friedman doesn't understand that an election will be coming up." It seemed clear that the three men had been discussing economist Milton Friedman's advice on a particular matter, that they agreed with his advice, but that the president would decline to follow it because of its possible impact on his 1972 reelection campaign. That persuaded me that the presidency should be limited to a single six-year term, long enough to give a president a fair opportunity to achieve his objectives but not so long as to enable him to inflict irreparable harm on the Republic should he prove a disaster.

In time, I came to realize that the temptation to avoid any position that might jeopardize reelection applied with equal force to members of Congress. By the time I left the Senate, I had blocked out a constitutional amendment that would have limited the president to a single six-year term and members of the Senate and House to two and six terms respectively— with, of course, appropriate grandfathering provisions to encourage disinterested votes on the part of those who would have to approve it.

The arguments against congressional term limits are that it takes time for newcomers to become effective legislators, that limits on tenure will increase the influence of staff over the work of Congress, and that term limits will result in the loss of the country's most capable legislators. It does indeed take time to master the arcana of congressional service, but the effects of careerism more than offset the fact that newcomers may require a couple of years to reach cruising speed. With respect to staff, a member of the House or Senate who is worth his salt will make sure that his own consists of individuals who know what he believes and why. Committee staffs will continue to exercise undue influence so long as members are too busy ensuring their reelections to devote adequate time to their committee responsibilities, a situation that my proposed reform is designed to alleviate.

The third objection is the most serious of them, but we should keep in mind that the lack of term limits also ensures the survival of a great deal of dead wood. One way to assess the reform's potential merits is to look back over the Senate's earlier years, when it was earning its reputation as the world's greatest deliberative body. During the nineteenth century, fewer than ten percent of the seven hundred individuals who served the equivalent of at least one term went on to serve more than two. Yes, life is much more complex today than it was in those times. It takes no longer, however, to learn the essential legislative ropes than it did then and it is worth noting that of the Senate giants of those days—Clay, Calhoun, and Webster—only the last served three terms. This suggests that a senator is able to make a significant contribution to his country's welfare within the twelve-year limit that I would place on senatorial service. While one may regret the departure of experienced legislators of real stature, their loss will be more than offset by banishing the careerism that today has compromised all too many of them.

There is a problem, however. In order to put term limits into effect, the Constitution would have to be amended, and that can prove an intimidating process. Our most recent amendment, which prohibits changes in congressional compensation from taking effect until after the next congressional elections, was proposed by James Madison in 1789 but wasn't ratified until 203 years later, in 1992. If it has strong enough support, however, an amendment can be adopted with surprising speed. In 1971, it took just 101 days for the states to ratify the amendment entitling eighteen-year-olds to vote.

I believe support for a term limits amendment may be strong enough to ensure its rapid ratification by the states. In the early 1990s, twenty-three states adopted limits on the time their own congressional representatives could serve. In 1995, however, the Supreme Court declared those limits to be unconstitutional. Nevertheless, according to a January 2013 Gallup poll, seventy-five percent of American adults continue to support limits. The problem is in initiating the amendment process.

In the normal course, a proposed amendment must be approved by a two-thirds vote of the Senate and House before it can be submitted to the states for ratification. To ease its passage through Congress, a congressional term limiting amendment should exempt current members of Congress from its effect, as was done with respect to the sitting president in the amendment that limited the presidency to two terms. In assessing the likelihood that grandfathered members of Congress might support an amendment limiting their successors' terms, one should keep in mind that Newt Gingrich's Contract with America, which swept enough Republicans into office in 1994 to give that party its first House majority in forty years, contained a term limits clause as did the Republican platform that fall. The following year, an amendment limiting congressional terms was supported by a majority of the House but failed to achieve the two-thirds majority required, so that was the end of it. If the necessary public support is there, however, political miracles are possible.

If members fail to be so enlightened, there is another route to a constitutional amendment. If two-thirds of the states choose to do so, they can call a convention to consider congressional term limits. As I noted earlier, twenty-three states had already adopted such limits before the Supreme Court declared them unconstitutional. If a convention should be called for the purpose, the wide support that exists for term limitations suggests that ratification by three-quarters of the states would not be out of the question. Given the damage done by careerism, it would be worth the try.

CAMPAIGN FINANCE REFORM

A January 8, 2013 article in *The Huffington Post* describes a meeting conducted by the House of Representatives Democratic Congressional Campaign Committee for newly elected Democrats just two weeks after the 2012 midterm elections. Its purpose was to give the newcomers nuts and bolts instruction on the basics of their new job. The article, "Call Time for Congress Shows How Fundraising Dominates Bleak Work Life," contains the following depressing passage:

> The daily schedule prescribed by the Democratic leadership contemplates a nine or 10-hour day while in Washington. Of that, four hours are to be spent in "call time' [i.e., fundraising telephone calls] and another hour is blocked out for "strategic outreach," which includes fundraisers and press work. An hour is walled off to "recharge," and three to four hours are designated for the actual work of being a member of Congress—hearings, votes, and meetings with constituents. If the constituents are donors, all the better.

Taken at face value, this means that these newly minted representatives are being urged to devote roughly half of their nine-to ten-hour workdays to ensuring their reelection rather than to the work they were elected to perform.

While the article quotes a former Virginia congressman as saying that the four hours assigned to fundraising might be "low-balling the figure so as not to scare the new Members too much," others suggest that less time is required, especially for those from safe districts. Whatever the hours, they represent a huge diversion from legislative work. Senators are also routinely reported as having to scrounge for money on a daily basis, and in the late 1990s two of them cited their disgust with panhandling as a major reason for their decisions not to seek reelection. In my own six years in the Senate, I did none of that. Although I attended some fundraisers when I was seeking reelection in 1976, I never once picked up the phone to ask for a contribution. That was the job of my campaign finance committee.

All of which raises the question: what can explain the dramatic difference between my experience and that of current members of Congress? The answer is the Supreme Court's decision in the 1976 case of *Buckley v. Valeo* in which I served as lead plaintiff. That case tested the constitutionality of the Campaign Reform Act of 1974's ceilings on what could be spent on congressional campaigns and on the amount an individual could contribute to a candidate ($1,000 at the time, a figure that has since been raised to $2,600). In rendering its decision, the Court equated money with speech, because these days it takes money to make oneself heard. As a consequence, the Court ruled that the limits on campaign spending violated the First Amendment's guarantee of freedom of speech, but it nevertheless accepted the $1,000 cap on individual contributions on the ground that the need to avoid the fact or appearance of corruption justified this limited constraint on speech. The Court made an exception, however, in the case of candidates contributing to their own campaigns, on the reasonable assumption that a candidate is incapable of corrupting himself.

What distinguishes the campaign finance issue from just about every other one being debated these days is that the opposing sides do not divide along conventional liberal/conservative lines, as illustrated by the individuals and organizations who joined me in bringing the case. What we had in common was that we were all political underdogs or outsiders. Although I was a United States Senator at the time, I had squeaked into office four years earlier as the first third-party candidate in forty years to be elected to the Senate. My co-plaintiffs included former Senator Eugene McCarthy, who had bucked his party's establishment by running a primary challenge effective enough to cause President Lyndon Johnson to withdraw his candidacy for reelection; the very conservative American Conservative Union; the equally liberal New York Civil Liberties Union; New York's Conservative Party; and Stewart Mott, a wealthy sponsor of liberal causes who had contributed $220,000 to the McCarthy presidential campaign.

What brought us together was the conviction that the 1974 amendments would effectively squeeze independent voices and political reform movements out of the political process by making it even more difficult than it already was to raise effective challenges to the political status quo. We believed that the restrictions imposed by the law were fundamentally flawed. At the heart of the First Amendment is the freedom of political speech. In today's world, it is incontrovertible that it takes money, and a great deal of it, for political speech to be heard. A healthy democracy should encourage competition in the political marketplace rather than increase the difficulties already faced by those challenging incumbents or the existing political establishment. Incumbents enjoy enormous advantages over challengers. These include name recognition, the use of the frank to communicate with constituents, automatic access to the media, and the goodwill derived from handling constituent problems.

Given this fundamental political reality, challengers who are not wealthy or celebrities in their own right must be able to persuade both the media and a broad base of potential contributors that their candidacies are credible. That requires a substantial amount of seed money. As I testified in *Buckley*, I could not have won election in 1970 if the $1,000 limit on individual contributions had been in place. Thanks to around $60,000 in gifts from a handful of individuals, my campaign was able at the outset to hire key personnel, print campaign literature, and rent a strategically located New York City headquarters. This caused the media to take my candidacy seriously and that, in turn, enabled me to raise (largely through mass mailings) the $2,000,000 required for a competitive campaign. Nor could Senator McCarthy have launched a serious challenge to an incumbent president without the more than $1,000,000 that was provided by fewer than a dozen early supporters.

In the wake of the Supreme Court's decision, we are left with a package of federal election laws and regulations that have distorted nearly every aspect of the election process. They have virtually driven grassroots action from the campaign scene because the rules have become too complex and the costs of a misstep too great. In 1970, when on campaign tours around New York State, I would run into groups that, on their own initiative, had rented storefronts from which to dispense my campaign literature, man the phones, and deploy volunteers. Today, supporters intrepid enough to engage in spontaneous action of that kind would be well advised to enlist the counsel of an election lawyer and accountant; and even then, they must be prepared to prove their independence in court. In the case of my New York storefront volunteers, the mere possession of my campaign handouts would have been cited as proof enough of collusion.

Today's reformers complain about the power of political action committees, and there is some justification for their concerns. PACs can have very specific objectives and they may condition contributions on a candidate's commitment to vote this way or that on future legislation. But those committees are prime beneficiaries of the restrictions placed on individual giving by the reformers of 1974. A citizen who would have contributed $25,000 to one or two candidates in whom he believes, but is limited to a gift of $2,600 to each, will find other ways to deploy the rest of the money he has earmarked for political purposes. The PACs provide a ready alternative.

There is general agreement that the current state of the law governing federal campaigns is unsatisfactory. The answer, however, is not to place further restrictions on the freedom of political speech but to reexamine the premises on which the existing limits have been based. In the first instance, dozens of recent races have demonstrated that money can't buy elections. The voters have the final say. What money can do is buy the exposure without which no candidate, however meritorious, has a chance. That is the major reason why sound public policy should not place artificial obstacles in the way of challengers trying to launch viable campaigns.

Second, while it is of course true that large contributions can corrupt, the likelihood that a candidate will be seduced by them is vastly overstated. The overwhelming majority of wealthy donors back candidates with whom they are in general agreement in the first place, and they are far more tolerant of differences on individual issues than are the PACs or other single-issue organizations to which a candidate will otherwise turn for necessary financing. It is also true that a major financial contributor will have readier access to a candidate he has helped elect, and with access comes the opportunity to persuade. But corruption only occurs when a legislator casts a vote that violates his convictions in exchange for financial support, and virtually every study of actual voting patterns suggests that that kind of corruption is too rare to warrant the distortions created by the present law in an attempt to avoid the appearances of impropriety.

Nevertheless, although large contributions can lead to corruption, the current requirement that contributions above $200 be disclosed provides a measure of protection. The opposing campaign can be relied on to publicize any gift that could give rise to an adverse inference and the public can then decide whether the contribution is apt to corrupt its recipient.

Disclosure, however, is proving to be a double-edged

sword. In his concurring opinion in *Citizens United v. FEC*, Justice Clarence Thomas described in chilling detail the organized harassment of individuals who had made contributions in support of a 2008 California ballot proposition to ban gay marriages. He concluded that he could not "endorse a view of the First Amendment that subjects citizens of this Nation to death threats, ruined careers, damaged or defaced property, or pre-emptive and threatening warning letters as the price for engaging in core political speech, the primary object of First Amendment protection" (internal quotation marks omitted).

Justice Thomas's opinion is fully consistent with earlier Supreme Court decisions. In the 1958 case of *NAACP v. Alabama*, for example, the Court held that the state could not compel disclosure of the NAACP's membership because of the harassment and worse that that could invite: "Inviolability of privacy in group association may in many circumstances be indispensable to preservation of freedom of association, particularly where a group espouses dissident beliefs." That reasoning surely applies with equal force to the freedom to support a particular position or candidate without fear of adverse consequences. Today's social media have given those consequences a particular virulence. In the case of Proposition 8, opponents created websites that identified its supporters and provided maps showing the location of their homes. This resulted in the mass harassments and property damage cited by Justice Thomas.

And the opponents have proven to have very long memories. Six years after the California proposition passed, they used the information that Brendan Eich, the newly appointed CEO of Mozilla Corporation, had contributed $1,000 in support of the proposition to organize campaigns of corporate harassment that forced Mr. Eich to step down.

Justice Thomas' concerns suggest an alternative to disclosure that would not merely address the fear that large campaign contributions could lead to corruption; it would eliminate the possibility. To this end, Congress should consider legislation requiring that all campaign contributions above a certain sum be made anonymously. This could be done by requiring that they be routed through a neutral third party such as a bank. To ensure anonymity, the law could impose a mandatory jail sentence for any disclosure of their sources. But whether one discloses contributions or insists on their anonymity, what makes no sense is to retain a set of rules that makes it impossible for a Stewart Mott to provide a Eugene McCarthy with the seed money essential to a credible challenge to a sitting president, or that makes politics the playground of the super-rich, who can finance their own campaigns.

The greater the government's involvement in our lives, the more important it is that participation in political debate be unhampered by artificial restraints. If caps on contributions to candidates are lifted, donors will send their checks directly to the candidates of their choice rather than to PACs. Incumbents will have no difficulty securing the money they need for their next campaigns without squandering precious time on fundraising telephone calls. At the same time, viable challengers who are not wealthy will find it easier to launch competitive campaigns because no side of the policy debates has a monopoly on money.

I therefore urge Congress to rescind the limit on what American citizens are allowed to contribute to candidates of their choice. I hope that its members' liberation from the odious chore of daily pleas for contributions will encourage them to adopt this reform even though it will help challengers raise more adequate war chests. A healthy democracy requires that each side of the political debate have a fair chance to be heard.

A FEDERALISM FOR OUR TIMES

[B]y the development of the principle of federalism,
[the American Constitution] has produced a community
more powerful, more prosperous, more intelligent, and more
free than any other which the world has seen.

—BRITISH HISTORIAN LORD ACTON

In 2013, when asked by the press where the Constitution authorized Congress to require Americans to buy health insurance, House Speaker Nancy Pelosi replied, "Are you serious? Are you serious?" As it happens, a few months later a very serious Supreme Court ruled that Congress could not do so although it did have the authority to impose a tax on those who failed to purchase the insurance. Speaker Pelosi's innocence of constitutional niceties is typical of today's members, and with some reason: the Supreme Court's constructions of the Constitution's Spending Clause have blurred the line separating federal from state responsibilities. As a result, it too rarely occurs to members of Congress that their legislative inspirations might violate our charter.

When I entered the Senate in 1971, I was among those who took federalism seriously. When a new measure was introduced for a vote, I saw little point in peering into my pocket Constitution to see whether the measure fell within one of the enumerated powers it had assigned to Congress. The federal government was already exercising too many unenumerated ones with the Supreme Court's blessing for a perusal of the Constitution's language to be of any help. Instead, I tried to put myself in the Framers' shoes. If the objective of a proposed bill was important and could only be achieved through national legislation, I would vote for it. Otherwise, I would oppose it as inconsistent with the principle of federalism. What I was doing unconsciously was to apply the rule of subsidiarity (a concept I had not yet heard of) in order to determine which level of government should exercise newly spawned duties.

Thus I had no problem with the federal government's assumption of responsibility for the environment. Air, water, and wildlife move across state lines. Airborne pollution generated in the Midwest can create health problems in the Northeast, and real estate developments in Georgia's coastal wetlands can affect fisheries along the entire Atlantic seaboard. It was clear that the effective abatement of pollution and protection of wildlife could only be handled at the national level. On the other hand, because states are fully competent to provide for the education of their own children, I voted against every education bill that came up for a vote, even when adorned with amendments that I had authored.

In order to ensure the survival of a healthy federalism, we need an easily understood and clearly stated test for determining the constitutional limits of congressional authority. That test is to be found in the Supreme Court's decision in the 1937 case of *Helvering v. Davis,* which challenged the constitutionality of the Social Security Act's provision of old-age insurance. The Court held it to be a legitimate exercise of Congress's power to provide for the general welfare because the insurance was "plainly national in area and dimensions," that "laws of the separate states cannot deal with it effectively," and that "[o]nly a power that is national can serve the interests of all." In so ruling, the Court has given us a simple, coherent standard for determining the legitimacy of Congress's handiwork: the laws it enacts must serve a purpose that can only be achieved through action at the national level. There will always be arguments as to when the line requiring national action is crossed, but that is true when determining the reach of other federal powers as well. It is this standard that distinguishes Medicare from Medicaid. Medicare is a package of medical benefits that attach to the individual wherever he might be. Only a national government can keep track of a mobile population. Qualification for Medicaid, by contrast, is determined state by state.

Helvering v. Davis also provides an answer to Justice Oliver Wendell Holmes' musings, in the 1920 case of *Missouri v. Holland*, over the scope of federal authority: "It is not lightly to be assumed that, in matters requiring national action, a power that must belong to and somewhere reside in every civilized government is not to be found." I question Justice Holmes' premise but the Court has provided an answer. In *Helvering*, it asserts that the authority to attend to those matters resides in the words "general welfare." What requires national action awaits discovery as an increasingly civilized Congress assumes responsibilities that the Constitution's authors could not have anticipated in the twilight years of the eighteenth century, responsibilities such as that of providing old-age insurance for a mobile population. What *Helvering* has done, in effect, is incorporate the rule of subsidiarity into the Constitution.

Unfortunately, the Court managed to muddy the waters in a five-to-four decision that it issued that same day. That case, *Steward Machine Co. v. Davis*, dealt with a provision of the Social Security Act that offered federal assistance in leveling the impact of various state unemployment compensation taxes. Because the states were at liberty to decline the federal offer, the Court ruled that the program did not coerce their compliance "in contradiction of the Tenth Amendment." It therefore held that the program was a legitimate exercise of Congress's authority to provide for the general welfare. As I have pointed out, that holding provides Congress with an irresistible invitation to focus on state and local issues, thus undercutting the distinction between federal and state responsibilities that lies at the heart of federalism. The practical effect of that decision is to apply one provision of the Constitution, the Spending

Clause, in a way that undermines another's guarantee of state sovereignty, namely the Tenth Amendment.

I hope the Supreme Court will find the occasion to review that precedent critically in the light of its unintended consequences, namely the explosion of grants-in-aid programs. In *New York v. United States* (1992), the Court held that Congress could not commandeer a state and require it to discharge a federal responsibility. Yet in *Steward Machine Co.*, the Court held, and continues to hold, that Congress may achieve by seduction what it has no power to compel directly. I cannot believe that the Constitution's authors would have condoned such a subversion of their carefully constructed allocation of governmental responsibilities. If the Court does review that case, it should affirm that Congress has no authority to induce the states to adopt programs or policies that it itself has no power to enact. The Court should also take the occasion to reiterate the simple, prudential test of the limits of congressional power contained in *Helvering v. Davis*, to wit: if a constitutional objective can only be achieved through federal action, Congress may do its will; if that is not the case, the states retain the exclusive authority to do theirs free of congressional inducements to do Washington's.

If the Court issues such an opinion, Congress might once again be persuaded to take federalism seriously.

Acknowledgments

It is astonishing that policy analysts pay so little critical attention to the costs and consequences of the grants-in-aid programs that account for so large a part of our national budget. The exception is Mr. Chris Edwards, of the Cato Institute, who has written important papers on the subject. Over the years, I have taken strong exception to a large number of federal grants programs, but it had never occurred to me to focus on the practice itself until I came across his analyses. I am indebted to him both for inspiring me to write this book and for marshalling much of the information that it contains. The book, however, would never have been written if my publisher and friend, Roger Kimball, had not encouraged me. I am also indebted to Charles Dameron, a student at the Yale Law School and an editor of its law review, for his invaluable research.

Appendix A

PROGRAM REDUNDANCY: A SAMPLING

The 2011 Government Accountability Office report on *Opportunities to Reduce Potential Duplication in Government Programs, Save Tax Dollars, and Enhance Revenue*, which I quote at some length in this book, cites some egregious instances of program redundancy (e.g., the 82 programs dealing with teacher training) but fails to identify them. In 2000, however, the GAO published a report titled *Economic Development: Multiple Federal Programs Fund Similar Economic Development Activities*; Appendix III of this document identifies six areas of economic development and lists, with comments, the federal programs and agencies involved in each:

- Planning economic development activities (9 agencies, 44 programs)
- Constructing or renovating nonresidential buildings (8 agencies, 29 programs)

- Establishing business incubators
  (5 agencies, 19 programs)

- Constructing industrial parks
  (6 agencies, 20 programs)

- Constructing and repairing roads and streets
  (6 agencies, 27 programs)

- Constructing water and sewer systems
  (7 agencies, 31 programs)

Appendix III of the GAO's 2000 report deals with programs in existence in 1999. The GAO's 2011 report indicates that redundancy remains an immense problem, and the resulting waste will be even greater as the amount spent in support of economic development increased from $8.7 billion in 1999 to $18.8 billion in 2010.

The following pages reproduce those portions of Appendix III in the 2000 report that deal with industrial parks and roads and streets, areas that fall so clearly within the competence of state and local officials.

Six Agencies Administer 20 Programs That Can Fund Industrial Parks

Industrial parks generally include a tract of land under the control of one entity that provides facilities for businesses consistent with a master plan. Industrial parks provide a wide array of economic development opportunities, such as manufacturing, research, warehousing and distribution, and service centers. Critical components of these parks include transportation, water and sewer, utilities, and telecommunications infrastructure. We identified six federal agencies that can fund industrial parks through 20 programs for various types of applicants. (See table 6.)

Table 6: Federal Programs That Can Be Used to Fund Industrial Parks, Listed by Agency

Dollars in millions

Agency/ program/ (catalog number)/ industrial park obligations for fiscal year 1999[a]	Applicants					
	Individual	Local	Nonprofit	State	U.S. territories	Federal tribal governments
U.S. Department of Agriculture						
National Forest/Dependent Rural Communities (10.670)		•	•			•
Rural Development, Forestry and Communities (10.672)		•	•	•	•	•
Community Facilities Loans and Grants (10.766), $1		•	•	•	•	
Rural Development Grants (10.769)		•	•	•		
Empowerment Zones Program (10.772)		•		•		

Program	1	2	3	4	5	6
Rural Economic Development Loans and Grants (10.854), $0	•	•	•	•	•	•
Appalachian Regional Commission						
Appalachian Area Development (23.002), $5	•	•	•			
Department of Commerce						
Grants for Public Works and Economic Development (11.300), $51	•	•	•	•	•	
Economic Adjustment Assistance (11.307), $11	•	•	•	•	•	
Department of Health and Human Services						
Community Services Block Grant/Discretionary Awards (93.570)			•			
Department of Housing and Urban Development						
CDBG/Entitlement Grants (14.218)		•				
CDBG/Small Cities Program (14.219)		•		•		
CDBG/Special Purpose Grants/Insular Areas (14.225)					•	
CDBG/State's Program (14.228)				•		
Historically Black Colleges and Universities Program (14.237)				•		
Empowerment Zones Program (14.244), $1				•		
CDBG/Economic Development Initiative (14.246)		•				
CDBG/Section 108 Loan Guarantees (14.248)			•			
Indian CDBG Program (14.862), $0						•
Department of the Interior						
Indian Loans/Economic Development (15.124), $0						•

aSpecific industrial park obligations were not available for all programs.

Source: GAO's analysis of program information.

USDA and HUD administer 15 of the 20 programs, while ARC and the Departments of Commerce, Health and Human Services, and the Interior administer the remaining programs. The table also shows that federal funds for industrial parks are available to various types of applicants. Each type of applicant is eligible for multiple programs. For example, local governments can apply for 12 programs, and states can apply for 12 programs. In addition, many programs provide funding for more than one type of applicant.

In analyzing the purposes of these programs, we found that 18 programs included the promotion of economic development as a program purpose, while 12 programs listed improving community and quality of life as a program purpose. We also found that programs with the same purpose often had the same eligible applicants. Eleven programs share the common purpose of promoting economic development and supporting a local applicant, and six programs share the common purpose of improving the community, improving the quality of life, and supporting a local applicant. Consequently, a local applicant wanting to promote economic development through the use of industrial parks could apply to the Rural Economic Development Loans and Grants Program; Rural Development, Forestry and Communities Program; Grants for Public Works and Economic Development Program; CDBG/Entitlement Grants Program; CDBG/Small Cities Program; CDBG/Economic Development Initiative; National Forest/Dependent Rural Communities Program; Economic Adjustment Assistance Program; or USDA's Empowerment Zone Program, Rural Development Grants, and Appalachian Area Development Program. Applicants for the Rural Economic Development Loans and Grants

Program generally must be electric and telephone utilities that have current loans with USDA's Rural Utilities Service or Rural Telephone Bank.

Assistance is provided in a variety of ways; however, almost all of the programs provide assistance through grants. Of the 20 programs, 7 are targeted to rural areas and 4 to urban areas. The obligations for fiscal year 1999 for the programs vary widely, ranging from $3 million to about $3 billion. Fourteen of the programs' obligations were for less than $100 million, 3 had obligations of $100 million to $1 billion, and 3 had obligations of over $1 billion. Agencies provided obligation information for fiscal year 1999 on industrial parks for nine programs. Two programs reported that $1 million or less was obligated for industrial parks, while three other programs reported no obligations. The Appalachian Area Development Program reported $5 million, the Economic Adjustment Assistance Program reported $11 million, and the Grants for Public Works and Economic Development Program reported obligating $51 million for industrial parks in fiscal year 1999.

Five of these programs require applicants to supplement the funds received with funds from other sources. In addition, one program—Rural Development, Forestry and Communities—may have negotiated cost-sharing arrangements. For the programs requiring funds from other sources, two programs require 20 percent or more in matching funds, two programs require matching funds of up to 50 percent, and another requires various matching percentages depending on the type of activity. In addition, one program provides a 90-percent maximum loan guarantee and requires that the borrower have 20 percent equity in the business being financed. Some of the programs provide greater assistance if applicants meet other criteria, such as if an area is severely economically depressed.

Six Agencies Administer 26 Programs That Can Fund Roads and Streets Activities

The development of roads and streets often promotes economic development. In addition, businesses consider a variety of factors, including the efficiency of transportation facilities, when making decisions to locate in a particular area. Six agencies administer 26 programs that support the development of roads and streets. As shown in table 7, federal programs for roads and streets are available to various types of applicants. Also, each type of applicant is eligible for funding for multiple programs. For example, local governments can apply for funding from 16 programs, and states can apply for funding from 15 programs. In addition, many of these programs provide funding for multiple types of applicants.

Table 7: Federal Programs That Can Be Used to Fund Roads and Streets, Listed by Agency

Dollars in millions

Agency/ program/ (catalog number)/ roads and streets obligations for fiscal year 1999[a]	Applicants					
	Individual	Local	Nonprofit	State	U.S. territories	Federal tribal governments
U.S. Department of Agriculture						
Schools and Roads/Grants to States (10.665)				•	•	
Schools and Roads/Grants to Counties (10.666)		•				
Community Facilities Loans and Grants (10.766), $11		•	•	•	•	
Rural Development Grants (10.769)		•				•

Program					
Empowerment Zones Program (10.772)				•	
Appalachian Regional Commission					
Appalachian Local Road Access (23.008), $3		•		•	
Department of Commerce					
Grants for Public Works and Economic Development (11.300), $28	•		•	•	
Economic Adjustment Assistance (11.307), $24		•	•	•	
Department of Housing and Urban Development					
CDBG/Entitlement Grants (14.218), $216			•		
CDBG/Small Cities Program (14.219)			•		
CDBG/Special Purpose Grants/Insular Areas (14.225)				•	
CDBG/State's Program (14.228)				•	
Historically Black Colleges and Universities Program (14.237)				•	
Empowerment Zones Program (14.244), $1				•	
CDBG/Economic Development Initiative (14.246)				•	
CDBG/Section 108 Loan Guarantees (14.248)					•
Public Housing/Comprehensive Improvement Assistance Program (14.852)[b]				•	
Public Housing/Comprehensive Grant Program (14.859)[b]					
Indian CDBG Program (14.862), $1					•

Department of the Interior

Program					
Road Maintenance/Indian Roads (15.033), $7					•
Indian Loans/Economic Development (15.124), $0					•
Economic, Social, and Political Development of the Territories and the Freely Associated States (15.875)			•		

Department of Transportation

Program					
Airport Improvement Program (20.106), $29	•		•	•	•
Highway Planning and Construction (20.205)		•	•	•	
Federal Transit/Capital Investment Grants (20.500)		•	•	•	•
Federal Transit/Formula Grants (20.507), $13		•	•		

aSpecific roads and streets obligations were not available for all programs.

bPrograms 14.852 and 14.859 were subsequently consolidated into a new program—Public Housing Capital Fund (14.872).

Source: GAO's analysis of program information.

In analyzing the uses of these programs, we found that 23 programs included road construction as a program use, while 22 included repair, reconstruction, or maintenance as a program use. We also found that the programs often had the same purposes and applicants. Thirteen of the programs could be used to construct roads and allowed applicants to include local governmental units. Consequently, as long as specific program requirements were met, a local community needing to construct a road could apply to one or more programs at ARC, USDA, Commerce, HUD, and the Department of Transportation. However, restrictions of specific programs distinguish one program from another. Such restrictions include a requirement that funding be used for rural areas, for areas with low- and moderate-income persons, or for areas in a targeted geographic region. For example, only communities in the Appalachian region could apply for the Appalachian Local Road Access Program.

Twenty-three of the programs that can be used to fund activities related to roads and streets provide funding through grants and three provide funding through loans. The obligations for programs varied widely, ranging from $3 million to over $3 billion for fiscal year 1999. Of the federal programs that we identified that funded roads and streets activities, most required no matching funds, while others required minimum matching funds ranging from 10 to 50 percent of the project's costs. For some of the programs, the required nonfederal matching funds varied on the basis of the area's level of economic distress, such as the area's level of poverty or unemployment.

Appendix B

STATE PER CAPITA INCOME
AND COST OF LIVING RANKINGS

	Per Capita Income		Cost of Living	
	$000s	Rank	Index	Rank
Connecticut	58.9	1	131.4	4
Massachusetts	54.7	2	121.9	8
New Jersey	53.6	3	127.9	5
New York	52.1	4	136.1	2
Maryland	52.0	5	116.8	11
North Dakota	51.9	6	101.9	16
Wyoming	48.7	7	95.8	29
Virginia	47.1	8	95.9	28
New Hampshire	47.1	9	120.0	10
Alaska	46.8	10	131.5	3
Minnesota	46.2	11	101.6	18
Washington	45.4	12	102.0	15
Colorado	45.1	13	99.8	20
Rhode Island	45.0	14	123.3	7
California	45.0	15	124.3	6
Illinois	44.9	16	95.7	30
Hawaii	44.0	17	158.3	1
South Dakota	43.7	18	99.5	21
Pennsylvania	43.6	19	100.8	19

	Per Capita Income		Cost of Living	
	$000s	Rank	Index	Rank
Nebraska	42.5	20	90.3	45
Vermont	43.0	21	120.1	9
Iowa	42.1	22	91.8	39
Delaware	41.9	23	104.8	14
Kansas	41.9	24	92.2	37
Texas	41.5	25	91.6	41
Wisconsin	40.5	26	97.3	24
Florida	40.3	27	97.3	23
Maine	39.5	28	110.4	12
Louisiana	39.4	29	94.6	31
Ohio	39.3	30	91.8	40
Missouri	39.0	31	92.7	34
Oklahoma	39.0	32	90.1	46
Oregon	38.8	33	106.4	13
Tennessee	37.7	34	89.8	48
Michigan	37.5	35	94.0	33
Montana	37.4	36	98.4	22
Nevada	37.4	37	96.4	27
North Carolina	37.0	38	96.7	25
Indiana	36.9	39	90.1	47
Georgia	36.9	40	92.3	36
Arizona	36.0	41	101.7	17
Alabama	35.6	42	92.3	35
New Mexico	35.1	43	92.2	38
Kentucky	35.0	44	89.0	49
Arkansas	34.7	45	91.5	42
Utah	34.6	46	91.1	44
West Virginia	34.5	47	96.6	26
South Carolina	34.3	48	94.4	32
Idaho	33.7	49	91.1	43
Mississippi	33.1	50	87.5	50

SOURCES: Per capita income: Bureau of Business and Economic Research—2012. Cost of living: Missouri Economic Research and Information Center: Cost of Living Series, 3rd Quarter 2013.

Index